GOOD
THINGS
HAPPEN
TO
PEOPLE
YOU
HATE

GOOD THINGS HAPPEN TO PEOPLE YOU HATE

Essays

Rebecca Fishbein

wm

WILLIAM MORROW

An Imprint of HarperCollins*Publishers*

HarperCollins books may be purchased for educational, business,
or sales promotional use. For information, please email the
Special Markets Department at SPsales@harpercollins.com.

FIRST EDITION

Designed by Fritz Metsch

Library of Congress Cataloging-in-Publication Data has been
applied for.

ISBN 978-0-06-288998-0

19 20 21 22 23   LSC   10 9 8 7 6 5 4 3 2 1

For Nana, who loved books

Contents

CONTENTS

GOOD
THINGS
HAPPEN
TO
PEOPLE
YOU
HATE

The Key to Success Is Never to Have a Dream

The worst place to cry in New York is Terminal B at LaGuardia Airport. I can declare this without hesitation because I have cried almost everywhere else in this city. I have cried on every subway line. I have cried (at least four times) for the duration of any route to any apartment I've lived in. I have cried outside the old Hot & Crusty franchise on Fourteenth Street. I have cried on the Brooklyn Bridge. I have cried at the Foragers grocery store in DUMBO. I have cried on the Brooklyn Bridge while carrying a salad purchased at the Foragers grocery store in DUMBO. I have cried at most bars in my neighborhood and outside my neighborhood, and I once cried so hard at the Meatball Shop they brought me a free ice cream sandwich.

So it is with great confidence that I declare LaGuardia's Terminal B—home to the American Airlines hub, several leaking ceiling tiles, and zero bars—the absolute worst place to drop tears in this godforsaken town. I learned this lesson on November 2, 2017, when I stepped off the bus at LaGuardia, checked my email, and discovered a maniacal billionaire was shutting down the beloved local blog where I worked. To make matters worse, he'd replaced the entire website with a stupid letter alerting readers to the site's closure, temporarily rendering the archives inaccessible. My job was gone. Six years of my work was, to my knowledge, erased. Not a single place served alcohol in the entire goddamn terminal. I was in hell.

·

I loved my blog job for a lot of reasons, not least of which was that blogging let me write about the news without having to do the scary work of reporting it. I am awed by real journalists who feel comfortable vacating their desks or kitchen tables to go outside and ask people questions. I am afraid of people and I am afraid of rejection, which makes actual reporting my waking nightmare. One of the worst assignments I had as a baby journalist was having to approach fifty people in bars and ask them their favorite New York hookup spots. I was twenty-two at the time, but I looked fifteen, and after three straight days of hounding drunk people all over Manhattan, all I had to show were a lot of rejections, a bunch of fake names, and an angry email from my editor suggesting "more thorough reporting in the future."

But blogging, for me, was all fun. Though I did occasionally leave my desk to report on City Council hearings, 7-Eleven grand openings, and other local newsworthy events, for the most part I got to riff on the news from the safety of my office. It was the golden age of internet writing, with the Gawker sites going strong alongside stalwarts like The Awl and The Hairpin, when young writers were encouraged to use and hone their voices. This was sometimes to the detriment of readers looking for real news, since when you're pumping out content at a rapid clip (at my most prolific, I was writing five to six stories a day), you miss facts, make mistakes, and tend to be less informed overall than a reporter who has hours or even days to research a topic. But for those of us who thrilled at coming up with a clever way to describe the intersection of the Cronut line and new iPhone line, this was the Time to Be Alive.

I was as lazy a student as I am an adult. I went to a private high school where everyone tried to murder one another to get into an Ivy, and then I went to a research university where everyone tried to murder one another to get into medical school. I majored in creative writing so I'd never have to murder anyone, and I started all my assignments the night before they were due. My junior and senior year, my roommates attentively joined study groups, didn't sneak into bars during finals, cleaned their bathrooms, and graduated Phi Beta Kappa. I was a fuckup who rarely made dean's list and once brought home an ex-Marine I'd picked up at a Ra Ra Riot concert. We did not understand each other.

At my blog job, though, it didn't matter that I studied too little and wasn't serious enough and tended to come into work hungover. The skills I built over years of pounding out essays last minute actually came in handy when it came to writing blog posts—I usually had maybe an hour to make 400 words sing, which wasn't all that different from working under pressure in the library. In the blog world, being a procrastinator was an asset. You had to think on your feet without time to prepare, and you had to love the rush that comes with publishing something decent in less time than it takes to defrost a chicken breast.

As an academic ne'er-do-well, I longed to find people who were equally good at just scraping by, and once I graduated, I discovered bloggers. Bloggers are great at coming up with quick ways to be mean, just like me. They like to get drunk and complain about how miserable they are, which is my favorite combination of activities. The bloggers I met and sometimes worked with were just as self-deprecating and self-destructive as I was, and after a few years of suffering through long hours, low pay, and carpal tunnel, I started to sense that maybe I wasn't an aberration so much as I fit a different type.

So here I was, desperate to find a place that accepted me for the sluggish human-who-refuses-to-talk-to-other-humans-except-through-a-computer that I am, and I found it in blogging. It took some uncharacteristic persistence for me to find it on a salaried basis (I spent a couple years waiting for the blog to hire me full time, probably because I kept mixing up *who* and *whom* and insisted on writing ALL CAPS posts about new zoo animals), but once I wedged my way onto the payroll, I was *in*.

It didn't take long for my blog job to become my identity. When it came to blogging, I wasn't just allowed to be me, I was *required* to be, which was a real treat for someone who'd spent the majority of her formative years being told the Real Her was too useless to function in the working world. "Let your freak blog flag fly," my editor told me, so I did. I wrote about Taylor Swift conspiracy theories and Banksy-themed Bushwick buildings and snakes that live in the toilet. I forced my thoughts about the Boy American Girl doll upon the world. I documented drunk subway rides and rode in a Hasidic holiday caravan and did yoga in a mermaid tail on the beach. I wore crop tops and hiking pants to the office. No one made me do math. I was very happy.

And there was this sense, too, that I was among family—that though my bosses and coworkers didn't share my genetic code, they did share the quirks and failings my real family couldn't quite understand. We were all maybe lazy, definitely funny misfits trying to find a home, and it was a miracle we had stumbled into one. But homes tied to turbulent industries tend to crumble once you've kicked your shoes off, and our comfortable abode was no exception.

·

When I entered digital media, I assumed the internet's plentiful bounty would spare me the bloodletting I saw at print publications, all of which seemed to suffer bulk layoffs on a weekly basis. The alt-weekly I worked at in Baltimore fired a wave of staff writers and copy editors three months after I started. In the first hour of my first day at my first post-college internship at a big New York City magazine, half the staff was laid off. But the internet, with its vast resources and young writers, felt like the safe place.

Like most twenty-two-year-olds, I was an idiot and wrong about everything. It wasn't long after I hitched my wagon to the blogverse that publishers discovered internet money was a lie. Facebook and Google changed their algorithms and fucked up everybody's numbers. Corporations realized they could run fewer digital ads and make the same number of sales. Hulk Hogan and Peter Thiel sued Gawker into oblivion.

The blog I worked at was independently run, but after all that madness, the owners decided to sell it to Joe Ricketts, a right-wing billionaire, bison superfan, and noted Donald Trump donor. Ricketts owned a hyperlocal news site called DNAinfo, and we, a gang of scrappy underpaid bloggers, were the cheap labor he hoped would ultimately bring down costs at his own site. We were moved out of our lovely little home in DUMBO to a sad midtown office where my crop tops no longer seemed welcome. Our management also had to slash jobs at the site we were joining up with, which made us *very* popular with our new coworkers.

At this point, digital media companies like Gawker and Vice had started unionizing. We had no legal protection and nothing but the promise of two weeks of severance if we were unceremoniously cut loose, a threat that seemed all the more likely under our new stewardship. So we joined forces with our new colleagues, unionized under the Writers Guild of America, East, and publicly announced not long after the merger.

It turns out rich people who haven't figured out their money won't spare them eventual death don't like to bargain with their underlings, and Ricketts threatened to can the whole company. We spent months wondering if we'd have jobs in the morning, or if Ricketts would shut us down on a whim. Which brings me to November second, at LaGuardia's Terminal B.

•

I thought digital media would be a good way to make money as a writer. I was incorrect. It turns out there is no good way to make money as a writer, and I should have listened to my grandfather and gone to law school. On the other hand, law school sounded (and still sounds) like a lot of boring work with a lot of boring people. Media is a lot of interesting work with people who like to bitch about it at weekly happy hours. But that's assuming you have work or beer money in the first place.

The thing about media is that if you have a staff job, at some point you'll probably lose it. Journalism is an industry in permanent turmoil, with publishers on an everlasting quest to balance profitability with quality work. They still haven't figured it out. It's possible they never will.

About a year before I lost my job, a popular website axed a chunk of their staff writers. A few months after that, yet another one laid off over a dozen on a single afternoon. A bunch of them showed up to a bar I was at, and I bought them drinks even though I didn't really know them. That's what you do when you're on a career track that's derailing in front of you. The assumption is that the last crop of unemployed writers will return the favor when it's your turn to get the carpet pulled out.

On the night my blog shut down, there was a big memorial meetup at a bar on the Lower East Side. I missed it, of course, because I was at the airport, crying and pacing the terminal and wondering if I should skip the stupid trip and go home. There was a lot of information to process. According to Ricketts's email, we were getting four months severance and four months of health insurance. This was a solid financial cushion, although months go by a lot faster than you would think; but at the very least, my panic attack in LaGuardia's Terminal B did not include a freak-out over how I would pay my next rent check.

Still, the place that had helped shape me was gone; and so, it seemed, was the work that had given me the first identity I liked. I was no longer Rebecca Fishbein, Staffer, Local Blog Queen, Slayer of Subway Delays. I was just a person standing by a rack full of $12 listless CIBO Express sandwiches, with no job and no purpose and no friends to buy me shots and hold me while I cried. I did, however, rack up, like, $200 in Venmo payments from journalists I knew and didn't who were clamoring to feed me alcohol. Solidarity is, as I said before, a real thing in a tempestuous working world.

·

I briefly considered fleeing the terminal to go get drunk on the Lower East Side, where my now-former coworkers and other journalists were gathering to toast my website goodbye. I did not want to miss my own funeral. But I decided against this plan. I had a friend waiting for me in Nashville and another meeting us on the way, and it would have cost me at least $400 to change my ticket. I couldn't afford that when I'd been employed, let alone having lost my job, so I boarded the flight.

I flew a few hours down south and took a cab to the hotel, where my friend handed me a takeout container filled with barbecue chicken. "I'm really upset," I told her. "You'll get another job," she said. I wasn't so sure. At least I had free chicken.

We walked down Nashville's famed Broadway, which was lined with neon lights like the Broadway back home. But unlike my Broadway, these lights were in the shape of cowboy boots, there were no child-kicking costumed Elmos, and all the pedestrians on the sidewalk were blond. My friends and I ended up drinking Budweisers and doing whiskey shots at one of the many country music bars, which I categorized as keeping up with my former colleagues getting trashed without me on the Lower East Side. At one point, I struck up a conversation with some dudes. "I just lost my job," I said to one of them, who was . . . tall? With a face? Hard to know.

"That sucks," he said. "I really loved it," I said. "That sucks," he said again. I noticed he didn't ask me what I did, a common refrain in New York and D.C. and maybe Los Angeles, but not always in places where your life isn't necessarily defined by your work. He had no further comment. I wondered if he would buy me a beer. He did not. I wondered if he would make out with me. He did not. People lose jobs all the time. I wasn't special.

I woke up the next day to a hangover and a hotel breakfast, and my friends and I shuttled to the Country Music Hall of Fame. I wandered through mocked-up cornfields from *Hee Haw* and Shania Twain photographs as I scrolled through my Twitter feed, which was full of journalists and readers lamenting my blog's death. My old colleagues appeared to be drinking themselves to their own deaths somewhere in Brooklyn. They were in New York, all together, and I was here, alone, staring at a mannequin wearing Jason Aldean's fourth grade basketball jersey. If this was the future, I didn't much care for it.

My flight back to New York was set to get me home

sometime Sunday afternoon, and I was desperate to meet up with some of my fellow fireds. But New York doesn't like it when you leave, and it chastised me by sending "wind" to delay my flight three hours. Once I landed, it took me over an hour to get *out* of LaGuardia, thanks to "construction," which I can only assume was the airport's way of doling out punishment for all the times I blogged about its crappy broken ceiling tiles. I figured I'd just go home and cry alone, but a friend was nice enough to meet me at the bar across the street from my apartment so I could cry to him instead. I cried about being scared about money and health insurance and bills and, just generally, the future, which at this point was a big amorphous unknown.

"What am I going to do?" I said, deep into my third glass of dive-bar wine. He couldn't answer me. I ordered more wine.

•

A lot of things happened after that, in a relatively short time span. Most of us found enough freelance gigs— reporting, blogging, copywriting, sponsored content, this damn book you're reading right now—to keep us from going bankrupt. The very companies that slashed staff jobs by the hundreds needed freelancers to write sans benefits, and we, starving scabs that we were, tended to take their places. We got disaster health insurance and Medicaid and stopped going to the doctor and maybe started biking with helmets, because we were young and healthy and could put off getting that mole checked out. The Ricketts money got deposited into our bank accounts for months, and by the time it was gone, we'd found more solid footing than we had on November second.

I staved off existential and economic despair by falling into some regular blog gigs, picking up some real estate writing, and publishing personal essays and dating advice pieces (LOL) in a bunch of publications I'd eyed back when I was exclusively tied to my old job. I missed being Rebecca Fishbein, Staffer, Local Blog Queen, Slayer of Subway Delays, but now I got to be someone else. Sometimes I was Rebecca Fishbein, Destroyer of Celebrities, Queen of Menstrual Cramp Killing Tips. Others, I was Rebecca Fishbein, Barer of Affair with Roommate in National Publication. And sometimes I was Rebecca Fishbein, Eater of Goldfish, Writer of Many Tweets, Taker of Many Naps. Freelancing is a roller coaster! But there was a certain satisfaction in knowing I could be whomever I wanted, and that my sense of self wasn't tied to a job that was out of my control.

•

After our website was shuttered, my friends at another blog, Death and Taxes, lost their jobs when it folded. In the summer, dozens of Gawker refugees who'd found a new home at Univision took buyouts when the company threatened mass layoffs. The Outline laid off all their staff writers. The *Daily News* canned half its staff. *The Village Voice* ceased print production, then killed the alt-weekly altogether. Though the gang of journalists I roll with once consisted of a solid mix of staffers and freelancers, by the end of that summer, almost no one had a job.

Journalism has always been like this. A few weeks ago I watched *The Paper* with a bunch of my unemployed friends, and the panic over ad sales and subscriptions and cost-cutting hung just as heavy in 1994 as it does now. It makes me wonder how long I'll stick this world out, if at all.

My friends who love to report miss the rush of the game, but for me, I miss my old home. I miss being young and hungry and convinced I'd found a spot for me forever, because it turns out *no* spot is forever, no matter how infinite a job seems when you're twenty-five and on top of your own tiny world.

•

A few months after Ricketts shut down our blog, one of the New York public radio stations decided to restart it.

Six months after that, I found myself sitting alongside my old editors at a bar on the Lower East Side. "I'm trying to convince you to come work with us again," one of them told me. "We want you to come back." It was a tempting offer, and not just because he fed me free beers and a Scotch egg.

My old life waved at me, carrying with it all the blog posts and local "fame" and secret office affairs that once comprised it. I could be the old me again.

But I didn't want all that old shit. You can't really go back. Maybe today I'll be Rebecca Fishbein, Drinker of Tea, Binger of *BoJack Horseman*, but last week I was Rebecca Fishbein, Celebrated Lady Blogger, and tomorrow I'll be someone else. And in six months, I'll be a whole other person. Maybe I will go to law school or flight school, or fight Nazis in the desert over a cursed biblical relic, now that they appear to be back. Maybe I'll do none of those things, and move home with my parents and dissolve into irrelevance and bankruptcy on their couch. But I know one thing for sure. Next time I go to LaGuardia, I'm bringing a fucking flask.

Real Men Will Disappoint You, Date Fictional Men Instead

I am so old, I saw the first *Star Wars* film in theaters. Not the OG 1977 version (good Lord, I'm not dead), but the 1997 Special Edition re-release. The Special Edition films are controversial among true *Star Wars* fans, in part because they were the first hint that George Lucas was a CGI glutton who would stop at nothing to let gratuitous effects ruin his legacy, and also because Greedo shot first.* But in 1997, I was in

---

*This is a long-standing point of contention in *Star Wars* history. In the original 1977 *Star Wars* release, Han Solo shoots and kills a bounty hunter named Greedo at the Mos Eisley cantina. But when George Lucas released the Special Edition films in 1997, he edited the scene so Greedo shoots first, making it look like Han was acting in self-defense. This is bullshit. Han is a badass. Han shot first.

second grade and had never before seen a Star War, so for me the magic was all new. My father took me to see *Episode IV: A New Hope* at the Lincoln Square movie theater on a school night, a special event since (a) he and I rarely went to the movies alone together and (b) I had never been to a movie on a weeknight. I was, at long last, a grown-up, and now I was going to see a grown-up movie.

I like to think of my childhood as Before *Star Wars* (BSW) and After *Star Wars* (ASW). I walked out of the theater that night a different person. I was still a weird, dumb little seven-year-old with big hair and a predilection for picking my nose and flicking the goo places, but now I knew about space. Space was a place with adventures and furry aliens and excitement. Space had loud guns, Carrie Fisher's fake British accent, laser sword battles, bad men with bad respiration, slimy slug gangsters, the power-converter-filled Tosche Station, and robot people wandering an arid desert planet. Space had everything. Most of all, space had Han Solo.

Han Solo was the first man to take hold of my body and soul. He was a cocky thirtysomething space smuggler with a searing wit, a secret heart of gold, and a little tuft of chest hair peeking out of his space shirt. I loved the way he walked and the way he flirted with Princess Leia (like a second grader, which really worked for me at the time), and how sad, frustrated, and hurt he looked in *The Empire Strikes Back* after the Empire tricked him on Bespin and forced him to face the electric torture machine. He tortured me, after all, so watching him take on similar pain was a matter of emotional equality.

It was a difficult relationship for the two of us, as he spent most of it battling the Empire in a galaxy far, far away, while I was on planet Earth learning how to write in cursive. Also, he was fictional. But that didn't matter to me. Han Solo was my first Man, and I spent many of my waking hours dreaming up stories about our tandem space exploits. I was certain that one day I'd meet a Man just like Han Solo in real life, and that he, too, would make life an adventure.

(Note that in these daydreams, Han Solo was my uncle, and I was his whiz-kid space niece whose secret weapon was a tiny handheld calculator I pretended was a mini-computer with internet access, because yes, I invented the iPhone. No, I have not yet received my royalties from the Jobs estate.)

My love for Han never truly waned, but as the years wore on, I developed a number of potent, if slightly less all-encompassing, crushes on celebrities and other fictional characters. These included, but were not limited to: Leonardo DiCaprio in *Marvin's Room*, Leonardo DiCaprio in *Titanic*, Peter Pan, one of the more boring Backstreet Boys, Johnny Depp as Captain

Jack Sparrow, Johnny Depp as Johnny Depp, Johnny Depp as Officer Tom Hanson on *21 Jump Street*. These infatuations were prepubescent and deeply chaste.

They were so chaste, in fact, that when I developed my next full-on obsession—Michael J. Fox, thanks to a family viewing of *Back to the Future* in the fifth grade—I inserted myself into the BTTF series as Marty McFly's made-up sister Maggie. (My understanding of love was limited to familial relationships.) I liked the way Marty looked in his plaid shirt and down vest, but I couldn't see myself in Elisabeth Shue's role as his girlfriend. I did, however, start waking up at six A.M. to catch reruns of *Family Ties* on CBS, and I threw a temper tantrum when my parents wouldn't let me rewatch *For Love or Money* because someone dropped an F bomb. (I surreptitiously managed to watch *The Secret of My Success*. It had a lot of sex in it, but I didn't get any of the references.)

I got over Michael J. Fox when I started middle school, preferring instead to imprint on the likes of Spike from *Buffy the Vampire Slayer* and the aforementioned Captain Jack Sparrow. Even those crush fantasies never made it past first base. Then one day I turned into a young teen and got my hands on the sexiest book I've ever read. My fictive love switched to lust at full throttle.

The sexiest book I've ever read has zero sex. It has

almost no touching. No one gets naked, not even once. The two romantic leads kiss a couple of times, but for the most part, they spend the novel looking at and flirting with each other, and more often, with death. It is chaste as a birdhouse collector convention, and pubescent me loved every minute of it.

The book is *Jamaica Inn* by Daphne du Maurier, who more famously penned *Rebecca,* after whose titular character I may or may not have been inexplicably named. My mother lent me *Jamaica Inn* when I was in ninth grade. At the time, I was obsessed with the first *Pirates of the Caribbean* film, which had been released that summer, and was desperate for anything depicting eighteenth- and nineteenth-century British vagrants with wild beards and bad teeth. "You'll like this one," my mother said, handing me her well-worn copy. "It's about pirates." She was right; I devoured it like a thirsty little monster. Which at fourteen is exactly what I was. But more on that in a minute.

This is one of du Maurier's deep cuts, so let me delve into the plot, which takes place in 1820. After her mother dies, twenty-three-year-old Mary Yellan leaves the farm where she grew up to move in with her aunt Patience at the Jamaica Inn, located on a lonely stretch of moor on Cornwall's northeastern coast. Patience's husband, Joss Merlyn, is the inn's landlord, and under his watch, the establishment has transformed from a respectable drinking hole into a gathering place for foul miscreants who wreck ships coming into the port to steal their wares. Mary's a bit of a goody-goody and spends much of the novel trying to expose her uncle's operation while simultaneously protecting her fragile aunt. She also befriends an albino vicar (a problematic character, though I can't get into that further without divulging too many of the novel's twists) and takes a lot of long walks in mud.

The real meat of the story, though, is that Mary strikes up a reluctant romance with Joss's younger brother Jem, one that ultimately changes her life and invigorated much of mine. Like Joss, Jem Merlyn is a criminal, but a benign one; he's a horse thief, and du Maurier makes it clear that he doesn't share his brother's propensity toward drunkenness and murder. But he's just enough of a bad boy that Mary can't help but be intrigued. He is also, per du Maurier's description, quite handsome and charming, with a quick wit and a good heart. Despite herself, Mary falls in love, as did I.

Jamaica Inn, which was written in the 1930s, was just accessible enough to introduce me at fourteen to that type of Gothic British romance, one rife with long looks and burgeoning desire, but no physical contact (or even first names). That kind of lust—stirring, unspoken, and certainly unacted upon—made more sense to me than the contemporary romances I saw played out on my favorite teen television programs, like *The O.C.* and *One Tree Hill.* Couples on TV stuck their tongues in each other's mouths and took each other's virginities. And though some of my peers were following suit, I was far more comfortable papering my bedroom with *People* magazine photos of the shows' actors than with mimicking their behavior in real life.

Plenty of young teens aren't ready to date, of course, but for me, the prospect was particularly chilling. I was in fifth grade when I hit puberty—the first in my class, in fact, at a particularly prudish Jewish day school—and while my mother and the American Girl body books explained what was happening to my outsides, nobody took the time to talk me through the hormone party raging *inside.* I was horny, and how. Every single non-relative with a penis set my nether regions aflame, and in a matter of months, my secret crushes turned from platonic to lascivious. But the ten-year-old boys I knew weren't ready for my advances, and the ten-year-old girls who were my compatriots weren't ready to commiserate or egg me on. I was left alone with my blossoming libido, and with no way to assuage it.

Since I had no friends or older siblings available to help explain all the emotions and urges jumbling within, I assumed I was some sort of damaged sex fiend, like the rapist in *A Tree Grows in Brooklyn*, or the creepy priest in the Disney interpretation of *The Hunchback of Notre Dame*. What little I knew about sex had informed me it was a thing only men wanted and women reluctantly handed over, which meant, of course, that something must be wrong with me. No one told me that teen girls want to have sex, too. So I did the only thing I could do with my newfound drive—I suppressed it.

It's hard enough to grapple with your hormones as a teenager. It's even harder when you hit puberty so early the stores you shop at don't sell training bras, so instead of addressing these urges, you stamp them into tiny, quiet shards and stick them someplace deep. The hormones I buried at ten stayed buried when I hit my teens, right when everyone else started experiencing and exploring their own. In ninth grade, my friends were starting to let boys feel them up during lunch period. But I was so afraid of accessing the feelings that had shamed me just a few years before that I refused to entertain the notion of going near a real boy, lest he figure out real quick that I was a freak.

By fourteen, I had traveled through time with Marty, sunk to the bottom of the Atlantic with Leo, and attended the Republican National Convention with Alex P. Keaton. And of course I'd flown from Hoth to

Kashyyyk to Bespin with my, uh, uncle Han. I knew how to imagine a relationship, but I didn't quite get what went into it.

Enter Jem Merlyn, fictional horse thief and throb of my celibate, um, heart. There is one scene about halfway through *Jamaica Inn* in which Jem tries to coax Mary into spending the night with him in the Cornish town of Launceston, but she's far too proper to give in to more than a few smooches. The scene is as explicit as the novel gets, which, for my repressed little body, was about the maximum I could take. Here's a passage:

"God, you're as hard as flint, Mary Yellan. You'll be sorry for it when you're alone again."

"Better be sorry then than later."

"If I kissed you again, would you change your mind?"

"I would not."

"I don't wonder my brother took to his bed and his bottle for a week, with you in the house. Did you sing psalms to him?"

"I daresay I did."

"I've never known a woman so perverse. I'll buy a ring for you if it would make you feel respectable. It's not often I have money enough in my pocket to make the offer."

(Reader, when I first read this, I shrieked.)

Like Mary, I was too scared to give in—not just to sex, which wasn't even on the table at that point, but to even admitting out loud that it was something I wanted, because I still felt sex was something I couldn't and wasn't supposed to want. To want in secret was transgressive enough. And unlike the boning teens on *The O.C.*, the sexless duo in *Jamaica Inn* was safe. Like me, the furthest they'd allow themselves to go was to want.

Star Wars taught me the world of men would mean adventure. *Jamaica Inn* taught me the art of pining. Jem and Mary pine but can't or won't have each other, just as I pined for Jem and couldn't have him.

As high school wore on, I dug deeper into works of fiction that predated *Jamaica Inn*'s virtuous romance. I pined for each sexless man I encountered: Mr. Darcy, Mr. Rochester, Pip Pirrip, all of whom, like my beloved Jem, were either untouched or untouchable. Occasionally I managed to convert that pining into coveting real boys from afar—as long as they didn't know I liked them, as fictional Jem couldn't know I liked him, I was still safe, from them and from myself. Of course, my proclivities matured with age, and by my senior year, I'd fallen in love with Jake Barnes of *The Sun Also Rises*. It was a decidedly more risqué choice, since he ran with a racier crowd than I was used to. But thanks to his war injury, he was still an ungettable get, and therefore a safe target for my silent yearning.

I'd like to say that when I grew up, I moved on from pining for fictional Gothic men and television doctors, and certainly, in most ways I did. I left *Jamaica Inn* when I left high school, and in college and adulthood, my hidden crushes became hookups, flings, relationships, and inevitably, exes. Each real-life person helped unpeel some of the longing I'd secreted away as a child. But the bad and good feelings that consume us as teens tend to sit with us a little longer than we'd like as adults. Even now I often struggle to move from wanting to having, in part because the wanting still feels so good and so safe.

A crush—a real live one, or even one in a book or a film or a show—is at its best when it's still just an idea or words on a page, when it hasn't yet had the opportunity to mutate from crush to crash. It hurts to pine from afar, but at a distance the hurt is in your control; once you spend the night in Launceston with someone, they'll know that you're a freak. The key, of course, is to find a crush who doesn't mind, and then once you move from wanting to having, you can cross over to keeping, which is the true goal of every good pine, whether it be Gothic, extraterrestrial, or solidly rooted on twenty-first-century Earth. I'm not there yet, but I'm working on it. In the meantime, every now and then I check back in with Han.

Sex Is Good for Your Complexion, but I'd Rather Have Acne

was at a bar one winter's evening when I got a text from an old friend of mine. "Ian is single now," she wrote. "He wants to go out with you."

Ian was a college buddy of hers I'd met a couple times, and it appeared they were out drinking together, since he then started texting me from her phone. From what I gathered from a jagged line of texts, Ian got dumped two hours prior, and he now wanted to meet up with me at nine P.M. one night that week in my neighborhood. "He won't be your boyfriend, but he's a good lay and you'll have fun," my friend wrote, after Ian and I had cemented our plans. "I hope you like whiskey shots," Ian wrote. And so it was settled: I was going on a Sex Date.

A Sex Date is very different from a real date, which usually consists of two parties trying to suss out whether they want to go on other dates, and perhaps eventually marry and divorce each other, over beers. A Sex Date is not about having more dates and/or weddings and babies. It is, as the name suggests, a date in which you meet up to have sex.

Though a Sex Date is not often explicitly stipulated when you're scheduling one, the parameters are thus: (1) You meet late. (2) You meet near someone's apartment. (3) You meet without having any intention of embarking on a relationship, unless that relationship solely comprises more sex dates and/or a trip to the doctor for an STI test, an oft and unfortunate Sex Date outcome.*

Ian's and my late-night plan checked all the Sex Date boxes. And certainly I was in the right state for a Sex Date. The week prior, the person I'd last been sleeping with had informed me that he'd wifed up with a hot former colleague, a revelation that rendered me immobile on my couch for a full twelve hours. They say the best way to get over someone is to put a bunch of

---

*A Sex Date may sound similar to a Booty Call, but they are very different. Unlike a Booty Call, a Sex Date feigns real-date-ness by starting out at a bar or restaurant. You don't spend money on a Booty Call.

new bodies between you and the old body you liked, and here was a fresh new body, begging to get me drunk convenient to my train stop.

Of course, just because you should want a new body doesn't mean you do, and I wasn't so sure where I stood on this upcoming Sex Date. Movies and television tell you it's easy and fun to let a cute stranger put their naked sex parts into your naked sex parts, but the movie strangers are usually played by Chris Pine, and they absolutely love that you prefer to lie there like an old mattress until they're finished. Chris Pine is perfect, and he thinks you're beautiful just the way you are. Real strangers don't like getting elbowed in the stomach when they try to cuddle you, or when you inform them, at two A.M., that the Q train is probably still running express if they hurry.

I've had far more non-magical movie sex partners than Chris Pines in my lifetime, and my body knows what to expect from itself during an ambivalent one-night stand. On the evening of the proposed Sex Date, the voice inside my vagina whispered that it was doing just fine without any new penile visits and did not feel particularly inclined to invite in Ian's. Couldn't we just stay home and watch the Winter Olympics instead? I considered its wishes, but then I saw a photo on Instagram of most recent ex-paramour and his hot successful new girlfriend at *Springsteen on Broadway.* I fed

Vagina Voice two glasses of pre-date wine and told it to shut up. Ian was cute, he wanted to bone me, and nobody else was blowing up my phone. Besides, I could always end the night with a hug if I wasn't feeling it. I am an adult woman, and I can sleep with or reject whom I please. Right?

Once you're seated opposite someone who's traveled from the Upper West Side to Prospect Heights to buy you shots, it's hard to send them home without some sort of thoughtful thank-you. We ordered more shots. We talked about bagels. We made out, because it seemed like the thing to do in the moment. When I asked, in my whiskey-and-wine haze, where we were going next, he said, "Your place," which now seemed fair. It was a long train ride home for him, after all, and considering the state of the NYC subway system, it would be nothing short of a local crime to direct him to the nearest stop. Also, he had shelled out for *shots*.

Ian called a cab to my place, and from there the night went pretty much as expected. There was some middling foreplay, intercourse, a mishap with a condom or three, some flailing around and teeth crashing. We'd both had so much whiskey there was about a negative 8 percent chance of either party reaching a climax. I passed out somewhere between "Do you mind if I just grab my vibrator real quick?" and the third snapped condom. In the morning, he texted me offering to pay for Plan B, and five days later I called in a prescription for UTI drugs. We never saw each other again. A beautiful relationship, indeed.

•

I am, as you've likely surmised, no stranger to bad sex. I had mostly bad sex in my early twenties, and considering the collective catharsis Women of the Internet experienced after Kristen Roupenian's "Cat Person" short story came out in *The New Yorker* in 2017, it wasn't just me. As evidenced by the young protagonist in "Cat Person," bad sex isn't necessarily violent or coerced, but you tend to have it just because you think you should, regardless of whether you want it or think it might feel good.

I was a late bloomer, and when I graduated from college with only a few drunken notches on my box spring, it seemed I needed to catch up. I didn't know how to, say, switch positions without kneeing someone in the chest; or to gracefully excuse myself to pee post-coitus to avoid the dreaded aforementioned UTI; or how to be on top without gyrating someone out of me; or frankly, even how to make sex feel good, for my partner or for me. Indeed, my early sexual experiences were at best boring and a little wet, and at worst downright excruciating, like someone was ramming a broom into my cervix.

Sex ed classes teach you that sex will riddle you with diseases and unwanted babies, but conveniently omit a lot of important stuff, like how to make it feel the least bit pleasurable. Pop culture teaches you that sex is a writhing, leg-twisting, candlelit thing you want, but doesn't explain why (or whether or not anyone observes fire safety by blowing out the candles when it's time for sleep). When I was young, the message I gleaned from teen comedies like *Superbad* and *EuroTrip* (an underrated early aughts masterpiece) was that men want sex and women want men to want them. Like many millennial women, I came of age watching *Sex and the City* reruns on E!, and thus was taught adulthood consisted of a rotating crew of short-lived relationships and one-night stands, with a couple epic romances tossed in for the sake of drama.

It was with this messaging burned firmly in my frontal cortex that I approached adulthood. Not that I felt like I was anywhere near it.

I am just under five feet tall and love Pixar films, and so I am literally childlike. I spent my first few years on the New York dating scene feeling childlike as well, while everyone around me grew up and got boyfriends and did sixty-nine without kicking someone in the face. But at twenty-two (and twenty-three and twenty-four and twenty-five, and sometimes at twenty-eight), I was still shocked that anyone who wasn't a registered sex offender would even want me to take off my clothes. To combat that, I decided to find out how many strangers were into seeing me naked.

At the time, dating apps like OkCupid and Tinder were starting to become popular, which made it easy to trick men into meeting up with me. Each date would go thus: I'd hit up a bar on the way to the chosen date spot for a shot of liquid courage, then make my way over, racked with terror that my prospective paramour would run once he saw my stubby legs slide off a barstool. Once we were trapped together, I'd pull out all the stops to force my date to fall in love with me. I'd crow about his favorite director, ask him questions about his hometown, pretend to care about his job, maybe touch his arm if I was feeling daring. Did I like him? Did I like any of them? It didn't matter. That wasn't the point. I was the dumb, useless child with something to prove, not them. They needed to want *me*—the rest we could work out along the way.

First and second dates were chaste, but if I made it to dates three and four, I had to psych myself into sleeping with these people or dump them. Those were the rules, after all, and if I broke them, my date would be disappointed, and I couldn't have that. I dumped most of them, but sometimes I didn't, in which case we'd go to dinner or to a comedy show, or we'd watch a movie at his house, and I'd drink heavily in preparation for fifteen or so minutes of clumsy, emotionless sex. Then I would leave, or if my date happened to be at my place, I'd make him leave. To spend the night with someone would require me to talk to him in the morning. I didn't know how to do that without revealing that I was a fraud. My dates thought I was sexy and experienced, just like them, but I was nothing but a child. These men were for practice. They were the experiences that would close the chasm between Girl and Woman that made me feel like I'd been left behind.

The thing about sleeping with people you do not want is that your body rejects them, something I revisited each time I woke up still smelling like a stranger's skin. I'd spend the next few hours drenched in shame over exposing myself inside and out to this person I didn't know or want, wondering if I could stand to let them touch me or even see them again. Over the following week, they'd weaponize my phone, attempting to will me back to them with cute texts I'd ignore. I rejected more than one by blocking his number. It was immature, but so was I.

Maybe I would have liked these men, had I known them. I wasn't trying to know them. I was trying to count them. In order for me to play with the big girls, I needed to rack up numbers and experiences, even if those numbers and experiences had me hyperventilating each time my phone pinged. I hadn't yet figured out that I didn't need to trick any strangers into liking me; that I could leave a date after half a beer if I wasn't into it; that no matter how confident, sexy, and experienced everyone else seemed, they were just as lost trying to mash their body against another body as I was. Instead, I assumed I was doing what everyone else was doing— putting myself out there, accommodating, *dating*.

This type of dating got me in trouble a handful of times, sometimes comically, sometimes not. Once I brought a date back from the Upper East Side to my apartment in Bushwick, but was so tired by the time we got there that I fell asleep before anything could happen. He left at three A.M. and took the train all the way back to Manhattan. He did not try to contact me again. Another time, a date could not, uh, *perform*, then collapsed on top of me in shame. "I have to be up *really* early," I said after ten minutes or so spent crushed beneath his torso. He took a full glass of whiskey with him when he left, glass included.

Once, almost on a dare, I brought home a man I met at famed Williamsburg hookup bar Union Pool. My roommate at the time paired up with the man's friend, and once we were back at our apartment, they retreated into her room while my chosen creature and I went into mine. When the lights were out, I realized I was alone with a stranger who was a lot bigger and more powerful than me. He didn't smell right. He didn't sound right. He hurt me when he handled me, and I didn't want him to be there. Unfortunately, he didn't want to leave. So I bit him, and not in a sexy way. "There's something wrong with you," he growled at me right before he fled. He left his muscle tank in my room, and the next morning I picked it up with a Swiffer handle and threw it in the public trash bin down the block.

These "dates" made up the majority of my sex life, until one day I discovered something spectacular: it is possible to have sex with people you like. Not only that, it's *enjoyable*. I made this discovery when I found myself in bed with a good friend whom I loved platonically, but maybe even a little more than that. The fallout from that encounter was messier and sharper than what I'd experienced with the strange men, but once I had good sex, the bad sex was much more difficult to tolerate, let alone welcome in.

A fun thing that happens when you stop letting yourself have bad sex is that you have much less sex altogether. A dry spell sucks at first—a few months into your newfound celibacy, you start thinking about banging your boss, your best friend, the big chair in your living room—but after a while your sexless life settles into a comfortable new normal, and there's a lot of good TV to keep you occupied. Six months and seven seasons of *Mad Men* later, you assume you'll never need to worry about a late period again. Then, following a few drunken hours at a dive bar, you'll find yourself on an express train going local and decide to pass the time by making out and subsequently going home with your travel buddy. The sex is good, so you keep doing it, and then you're dumped, fast as it started. Now you'll have to start all over. And that's how you end up on a Sex Date.

•

Other people seem to enjoy one-night stands or taking lovers or having neighborhood slam pieces they call up when the mood strikes. It is fine to be one of those people, but I am not and I never will be. One of the few things worse than no sex is sex you don't care about. But one of the things I didn't know, back when I welcomed bad sex, was that I didn't have to have it. Single women are constantly made to feel like their lives are missing something if they're not getting any, which is one of the things that tricks us into having sex without first asking ourselves if we even want it. Not to mention single women are reminded all the time that they can't find love because they're not open enough, or they're too picky, or they're not putting their best foot forward, which is sometimes how you get stuck (literally) letting a person in when you'd rather shake hands instead.

A friend of mine who got out of a four-year relationship asked me recently if Tinder was still "sex crazy," because the last time she was forced to date around, it was hard to get out of sleeping with someone if she didn't want to, since that was the going market rate. To go four dates without banging a prospective paramour risked them dropping you for someone more obliging. To say no was to risk their not liking you. To turn someone down—because you didn't know them, because you weren't sure you wanted them, because five drinks weren't enough to make you ready to take your clothes off in the dark— meant you weren't trying hard enough, and so the fact that you were single was all your fault.

In theory, women have agency when it comes to dating and sex. And it is still (theoretically) a crime to force someone to sleep with you when they say no. But it is hard, when you're in the moment, to remember that you don't have to kiss someone when they ask or lean in for it, or get in a cab with them because they bought you shots, and that pulling away from someone you do not want does not mean you will pull away from someone you do. You are not single because you will not settle for a night of bad sex with a stranger. You are not falling behind. The sexual revolution liberated women, but liberty is being able to say yes or no to sex with whom you please, not having to fuck every man who swipes right so you don't die alone. Dying alone is better than signing up for a lifetime of Sex Dates.

•

It's been four months since the Sex Date, which means I'm four months into my current bout of celibacy. I've managed to pass the time by watching *The Great British Baking Show*, and mostly I'm doing just fine, save for a rather elaborate occasional fantasy involving a barista at my local coffee shop and his mermaid tattoo. No sex and/or dating leaves me lots of time to get to know myself better, like what dinners I prefer to microwave or which vibrator setting will put me to sleep. You save a lot of time and money not worrying about shaving or showering, or about having to wash your sheets.

The other day, though, I opened up one of my dating apps out of curiosity, or maybe habit. I discovered something shocking: my winter Sex Date had just sent me a message. "Hey, how's ur summer going?" he wrote.

He had no idea we'd met.

He'd been inside me.

He'd forgotten me.

We are all each other's pawns in this game of broken condoms.

Don't Cry Over Spilt Milk, Have a Full-on Breakdown

I was nineteen the first time I lost my mind.

The summer before my sophomore year of college, I worked as a counselor at a day camp for rich kids. Two months of breaking up sticker-book fights in the baking Westchester sun had bleached my hair golden, and when exactly one (1) man on the street shouted, "Hi, blondie!" at me, it became clear that lighter hair upped my attractiveness level from Little Jewess Annie to Person of Perhaps Fuckable Age. This hypothesis was verified in the fall by the thicker-than-normal throng of collegiate boys clamoring to make out with and summarily reject me. But all things must die, even already dead cells, and by early spring, my hair had returned to its normal unremarkable brownish red. I, of course, was devastated. So one sunny day in April, I decided to spray a friend's Sun-In in my hair and spend the day outdoors.

For those of you who are lucky enough to be unfamiliar with this demon product, Sun-In is a popular hair lightener from the hair-healthy days of the 1980s. According to the sales pitch, a few quick sprays of the chemical concoction will "bring out your natural highlights just like the sun—only faster!" In reality, Sun-In is pure hydrogen peroxide, and about as good for your hair as pouring gasoline on your head near a campfire. The smiling blond model on the front of the bottle has clearly never touched the stuff, because when I washed it out of my hair that night, ready to be dazzled by my newfound resemblance to Reese Witherspoon, I discovered that my typically turbulent curls had deflated to a sad stringy, frizzy mess. They were also orange, a color that didn't pair well with my face, which turned fuchsia the instant I started screaming.

After a half-hour tantrum, I went to sleep, hoping my now-frazzled hair would settle overnight. In the morning, it actually looked worse. I googled "how to fix Sun-In," but as anyone familiar with Yelp reviews can attest, the internet is where the sadists of the world go to freak out everyone else with worst-case scenarios. Instead of finding helpful tips for hair resurrection, I found horror story after horror story documenting other people's Sun-In disasters. "Sun-In made my hair snap off!" one person screamed in a product review. "It's been a decade since I used this product, and my hair has *never* been the same!" shrieked another. "I HAD TO SHAVE MY HEAD AND WEAR A WIG," bellowed a third. It now seemed that Sun-In had affixed itself to my genetic code, cursing any and all of my descendants with ruined curls.

The hair forum deep dive tipped me from freak-out to full-scale mental breakdown. I could not sleep. I could not eat. I could not concentrate on my final exams, which took place only a week or so after the Sun-Incident. I took hundreds of photos of myself from all angles, checking to see how my new hair measured up against its pre-Sun-In iteration. I read even more message boards and product reviews detailing horror stories about triple-split ends and damaged follicles. I compared virgin strands of hair I found stuck on my sweaters to the Sun-In-fried strands on my head. I researched wig shops and doctors who did hair transplants. I wrote a treacly ode to my hair for a poetry class and dramatically read it aloud to the other students. "I watch my hair swirl down the drain / As I dream of straight, silky hair I'll never have and never know," I intoned. My classmates said the poem was "very funny."

To me, my hair looked like it belonged atop Julian Glover's decomposing corpse at the end of *Indiana Jones and the Last Crusade,* but to everyone else, my appearance was more or less the same. My friends were baffled. "You look fine," they said as I sobbed on our dorm room couch. My parents, unsettled by my hysterical phone calls, drove from Manhattan to Baltimore. They took me to a famous crab-cake place and tried to get me to eat. "It's just hair," my mother said, watching me dissect soft-shell through tears. "Nothing a good deep conditioner can't fix."

But rationality couldn't set my brain right or stop the spinout. Which, as it turned out, was imminent. In fact, the building blocks for a full-on breakdown had been quietly stacking for months.

•

The thing about losing your mind is that it happens when you're not paying attention. Depression is like a bedbug infestation—you keep waking up with bite-sized welts of self-doubt and sadness that at first you rationalize away, tricking yourself into believing you're not sleeping enough or are undercaffeinated or just have a teeny case of the blues. Then one day you can't get out of bed. That lasts for a week. Now you've got a problem.

•

My brain's slow collapse began, as all bad things do, with adolescent heartache. The fall after my hair turned blond, a boy I liked made out with me for two months before dumping me for a friend of mine. She had been offering counsel on this tenuous relationship before sweeping him off his feet. This kind of betrayal is bad enough, but it was coupled with some minor psychedelic drug experimentation (this boy liked drugs, so I did, too), and while I have no idea if the strange chemical concoctions we took actually screwed with my brain, for a time they did seem to reorganize the way I saw patterns—on the ground, in the light, and most important, in human behavior.

Some experts say gut feelings come from your brain recognizing patterns faster than you can consciously process them, instead squirting out a few drops of dopamine so you can sense irregularity or danger before it takes corporeal form. My newly sharpened mind had me convinced well in advance that the girl who stole my make-out buddy was going to do it.

When I voiced my paranoia, both to her and to my other friends, they told me I was nuts.

"I'm also so incredibly jealous of the fact that he and Emily keep having all this bonding time," I wrote in my journal one day. "I have this stupid irrational fear that he's going to realize she's so much cooler than me and fall desperately in love with her."

The next day:

jesus christ i'm fucking crazy.

i need to get out this moment of crazy right now before it engulfs me.

I'M SO WORRIED THAT HE WILL STOP LIKING ME AND WILL START LIKING EMILY INSTEAD

EEKAACKEEEEKAAAAAACK WHY WHY WHY WHY WHY would this bother me so much?

And the next:

i'm sure emily's upstairs with the boys now.

it's funny how the second i introduced her to them i felt like i'd made a mistake . . . i really didn't want her to come up with us that night. i really did want to keep them separate from her.

(Note that a very good exercise is rereading your journal entries from your teen years and trying to stop yourself from jumping out a window.)

Maybe I subconsciously saw how they looked at each other or talked about each other. Maybe I saw him touch her arm or watch her walk away. Maybe I sensed I wasn't actually happy doing drugs and playing video games with his friends, but stuffed down that dissatisfaction in favor of snagging a boyfriend. Maybe I suspected the panic I experienced each time I stood outside the door of his dorm room, trying to put on the mask that made me a person he liked, wouldn't be sustainable in a long-term partnership. But it was easier to blame inevitable fate and misfortune than to admit this wasn't what I wanted, and my fragmented synapses convinced me that I could sense bad things before they unfolded.

Bad things, it turned out, were everywhere. Not long after my friend swiped my paramour, another friend's father had a heart attack. Had I sensed it? Not that I recalled, but on second thought, my stomach *had* felt a little funny that morning. A roommate's relative was killed in her car by an oncoming driver. Had I known? Come to think of it, I *had* had a headache that week. I recalled an episode of the Nickelodeon show *Are You Afraid of the Dark?*, in which a cursed camera could snap a photo of a subject and predict its gruesome destruction. Was I that camera? Probably not, but certainly I was something.

•

In its early stages, as depression starts to seep in, everything is tinged with gray. You are still you, and your friends are still your friends, and your life is still your life, but it feels muddy and overcast, like you've relocated to the Upside Down or Seattle. Food starts to taste like air. Laughter is canned. You wake up and walk around the world like you're wearing weights on your arms and your chest and your back, and you start to wonder if things will always be this heavy. Still, you are fine, you say.

•

It turns out a great way to worsen a brain splinter is to study the skeptics. When I returned to school for the spring semester, I enrolled in a class on the history of modern philosophy. I showed up to only about 40 percent of the lectures, but on the occasional moments I peeled my eyes away from Solitaire, I took an interest in the works of skeptics like Spinoza, Descartes, and Hume. As a child, I had often lain awake at night pondering whether anything existed outside my own head (as normal children do), and so when I read about the cogito—*cogito, ergo sum*, I think therefore I am—my already warped little cerebral cortex latched on. Sure, if I imagined my friends betraying me, it might come true, but did it even matter if they weren't real? Who gave a shit about grades if they were just a figment of my imagination? If my parents died suddenly, who's to say they weren't hallucinations to begin with?

I floated on this false theory, wondering if I was just existing in a real-life version of the Matrix, my body pumping blood into a machine in an unknown robot-run dimension. Time started speeding up, sending me hurtling through the weeks and months faster than it used to, as if I were living inside a movie montage instead of real life. I was having trouble hanging on to minutes, and I started to wonder if I was even who I thought I was, if I was indeed Rebecca Fishbein, age nineteen, sitting in a dorm room in Baltimore, Maryland. I was just under five feet, with curly hair—for the time being, at least—and blue eyes and slightly blurry eyesight I refused to correct with contacts. I had two parents and a sister and, most of the time, a midterm due. These were the facts. This was my blueprint. Wasn't it?

•

Anxiety takes the gray of depression, turns it red, and twists the edges, speeding up your heart rate and making your hands shake. Anxiety doesn't just make you sad, it makes you scared, without permitting you to pinpoint a cause or possible solution. Anxiety warps your brain, inserting dark corridors into your future and packing them with threats. When you are anxious, you are always unsettled, no matter how much reading of online forums or deep breathing or crying into the phone you do. If you're not sure what specifically is spiking your adrenaline, then it could be anything, which means danger lurks from all possible angles.

•

Just a few weeks before the Sun-In-cident, my oldest friend's father died of complications from cancer. I happened to be back in New York for the weekend, where I was visiting a friend of a friend in Astoria, chain-smoking cigarettes and drinking tequila mixed with vodka (tequila and vodka—try this at home, kids, and then vomit all over your home!). I woke up with a vicious hangover and a voice mail from my friend with the news. I helped her buy a dress, slept in my childhood bedroom, went to the funeral, and cried on the train back to school.

And so here I was, losing my mind and track of time and dreaming of my own father going into the ground in a box. Thanks to the philosophy class, I wasn't sure if anything existed outside my shattered little head, but I did know that what I had, I could lose at any moment. The people I loved would one day be gone. The things I knew could change in an instant. They could be taken from me and never returned. And my hair could turn orange and never look normal again.

•

The problem with ceding your grasp on reality is that you don't know it's happening, because to you, everything feels quite real. You think your hair is falling out when it's not, because your brain is broken and won't tell you the truth anymore. You think your parents will die in a car crash on their way to pick you up from school, because that's what your brain is threatening will happen. You think time will start moving so fast you won't be able to see it, because your brain has sped up the clock. You think there's no point in staying alive, because who can live without a functioning brain?

•

Unlike people, scorched hair can usually be resurrected, and when I got home after the semester ended, I got a very expensive haircut. The stylist held my overdried curls in his fist and made a face. "It's horrible," he said before chopping off the deadest of the dead ends, then dunking my head in what felt like a vat of hair mask. Relief at last. The cut helped kill the frizz (the orange tinge stuck around for months), but it didn't quite put my brain back together, so I started seeing a therapist. We'd meet once a week at her Upper West Side office, where I'd spend forty-five minutes listing all my physical ailments. "I think you think too much," she said, after six weeks and $300.

I'd like to say that the therapy fixed me like the cut fixed my hair, but it turns out depression can't be snipped away as swiftly as dead ends. My therapist told me to email her, but I never did. Instead, I went to Rome for my fall semester and let thin men holding hand-rolled cigarettes psychoanalyze me. (*"Bella*, don't be sad, drink more wine!"*) After four months in which I exclusively consumed al dente spaghetti, my brain felt back to normal, maybe because I was distracted abroad, or because it was good for me to be taken out of my environment, or because the passage of time had given my skewed inner chemicals a minute to settle, or because gelato has some kind of supernatural healing power. Either way, by the time I got back to school that January, I felt like my old self again.

But that "old self" still had some sadness lingering beneath the skin, like a pimple trying to push itself out of a clogged pore. The myth of depression is that it's something that gets better, when really it's just something that lives inside you all the time, sometimes dormant, sometimes not. My Sun-In breakdown might have been the most extreme manifestation thus far of whatever weird shit was swirling inside me, but the weirdness had poked its head out from time to time in my past and would certainly pay me sporadic visits in the future. It's hard to stop feeling sad when you hate yourself, and it's hard to stop hating yourself when you're always feeling sad.

When I was twenty-five, I would suffer a spate of sadness so extreme I feared I'd get drunk and try to jump in front of a subway, so I went back to therapy. Finding that marginally helpful, I stuck with my therapist for a little over two years, until my health insurance changed and I didn't have the money or the willpower to continue. Then I slid into a fun period in which I frequently cried at bars, which was great for my friends and for all the strangers who wanted a nightcap but got my hysterics instead. Then, too, I wondered, late at night as I waited (and waited, and waited) for the train, if one day I'd be just the right amount of sad and just the right amount of drunk and take the leap. I considered this without any intention of following through, but when you've got the darkness in you, you can't help but flirt with the idea of doing something that might expel it into the world.

For example, a few months ago I went to the beach and a friend offered me a bottle of something to spray in my hair. "It's Sun-In," she said.

I did consider it—for a second.

Honesty Is the Best Policy, but Lying Will Give You the Life You Want

The other day, I was at my parents' house "work-ing" on this very "book" when I decided to take a look at some of our home movies. A few years ago, my folks burned tapes of me and my sister to DVD, and they're fun to revisit, unless they were taken when I was in middle school, and then I have to text my therapist. On this particular video-watching occa-sion, I sped through clips of me as a baby—featuring about a week's worth of footage of me taking cotton balls out of a bag and throwing them on the floor—and landed on one from August 1992, filmed at the Dutchess County Fair near my grandparents' house in Upstate New York.

In the video, I'm about a month away from turning

three, and I am fascinated by the fair's petting zoo. I did not grow up around animals. I never had any pets, and the only real contact I had with wildlife were glimpses of rats going home to the sandbox. On tape, I seem a little scared of the farm animals, but then a couple of fair workers show me a goat and let me pet it. I am overjoyed. I am elated. I am the happiest I've ever been. "At home, I have a zebra!" I tell the workers. I am, of course, lying.

They say active imaginations are a sign of intelligence. If that's true, I was the smartest fucking child in the world. I loved to make things up. I pretended the heroine from *Beauty and the Beast* was my big sister, spinning the tale so convincingly a friend's parent asked my mother about her "older daughter, Belle." I told a schoolmate I had two dogs, a cat, and a rabbit, even though the only life-form my mother let into our home was a jar of pond scum I cared for as part of my second grade science class (and even then she worried it might scuff up her floors).

I spent an entire summer at day camp claiming I had already turned seven when really I was only six. I told my friends I was a professional actress and was going to Florida to star in a production of *Romeo and Juliet.* I bent a paper clip, put it in my mouth, and told everyone it was a retainer. I started a detective agency, which consisted of my "solving" the crimes taking place in my classroom. My teachers couldn't understand why everyone's lunch boxes kept going missing. It was because I was stealing them. I solved the mystery!

I told all these lies because I was young and theoretically didn't know better, even though I absolutely did. I worried all the time that people would catch me making falsehoods, that they would hate me and stop being my friend. I worried they would tell my parents and make them stop loving me. I worried lying would ruin my life. But I couldn't stop doing it.

Lest you think compulsive lying was just a cute childhood habit, it did not break with age. If anything, as I got older I got better at lying, and my lies became both more believable and more significant. Every instance that dumped new people at my feet—summer camp, high school, even college—was an opportunity to spin a new lie, to make myself into a new human. I lied about dumb things, like cousins I didn't have and neighbors I'd never met. I lied about parties I'd never been to and cool friends that didn't exist.

And I lied about boys—people I said I'd kissed but hadn't, things I said I'd done but was afraid to do for real. Teen boys, it turns out, don't care much for unrepentant sarcasm and baby fat, and in high school I couldn't pay a dude to touch me (not to mention I was usually fixating on boys who weren't interested in me, not that that changed in adulthood). I have fond memories of a particular school event at which I thought a boy in my class was trying to dance with me, but really he was trying to distract me so his friend could mack on the girl to whom I'd been clinging. High school was always that beautiful. But when I made up stories about my sexual prowess, it didn't matter that I spent most Friday nights babysitting and/or creating complicated family structures on *The Sims.* While my friends were getting drunk and making out with boys at parties, I was, too. But these were parties they weren't invited to and boys they didn't know, since I fabricated them. I refused to get left behind, even if I was catching up only in my head.

•

Psychiatrists say compulsive lying stems from a slew of psychological problems, including borderline, antisocial, and narcissistic personality disorders. The interesting thing about compulsive liars is that though medical journals refer to them as "pathological," they tend not to lie for their own benefit. They're not trying to cheat their way into a job promotion or wave off a parking ticket or trick someone into hopping into bed with them. Rather, this kind of habitual lying works as a shield for people who believe they are not enough as they are. Instead of presenting the world with a person they hate, they present the person they want to be.

Liars are having a moment. This year, we have been inundated with stories about scammers and grifters who spun lies so convincingly they got smart people to throw fortunes at them for elaborate, impossible schemes. The story of Billy McFarland's fraudulent Fyre Festival—in which he managed to swindle $26 million out of investors, not to mention unpaid labor from workers on Great Exuma island in the Bahamas—was so wild it warranted competing documentaries from Hulu and Netflix.

Theranos CEO Elizabeth Holmes has been the subject of a book, a podcast, an HBO documentary, and an upcoming film starring Jennifer Lawrence after reportedly convincing investors to give her hundreds of millions of dollars by falsely telling them she'd spearheaded technology that would revolutionize healthcare. Anna Delvey, the so-called Soho Grifter, who allegedly posed as an heiress to get hotels, restaurants, and socialites to unwittingly fund her lavish lifestyle, is getting a Shonda Rhimes–helmed television series. People are fascinated by these liars. They want to know how the McFarlands and Holmeses and Delveys of the world manage to keep up with their grifts, and why they're so determined to spin these webs of lies that are sure to tangle and choke them.

I don't know these people, and though I pride myself

on the extensive number of *Psychology Today* articles I have read in hopes of diagnosing myself with primary psychopathy, I am not a professional armchair therapist. I would also like to think that sporadically inventing high school parties and fictional sex partners is less problematic than claiming you'd come up with a way to have blood pinpricks reveal cancer diagnoses. But a thing about compulsive lying that I have learned after years of living within its grip is that if you do it enough, you start to believe some of your own stories.

When you create your own canon, it can attach itself to your life like a ghost appendage, and things that don't exist feel like they do. You start forgetting what happened and what didn't. Did you kiss that boy, or did you tell yourself you did? Are you sure you don't have a dog and a cousin named Sam? Was it you who lost your virginity on this date to this person, or was it the alt-you, the cooler, braver version who lives in a dimension powered by your mendacious wish fulfillment?

•

My lying slowed down when I graduated from college and moved back to New York. In the Adult World, there were no rules and no deadlines and no honor-roll roommates judging me for getting fucked up on a weeknight, and so life outside my head started to feel interesting enough to stand on its own. The new me smoked weed on the street, and went to DIY shows in Williamsburg, and knew people with tattoos in bands, and stayed out until four A.M. with her store manager while he rolled her cigarettes. The new me tripped on MDMA at house parties, and once let a strange man bite her on the face at a bar. The new me was wild and scary and brave, and she was beginning to feel okay about existing in the world as she was, even if the current me cringes to remember some of her exploits.

But slowing down is not stopping completely. I am not good at kicking bad habits. I sucked my thumb until I was in the second grade, and I have the buckteeth to prove it. Even in Adult World, lies managed to dribble out of my mouth when I didn't want them to, particularly if booze was involved. I'd entertain new friends at bars with stories about dates I hadn't had and lovers I hadn't taken, then wake up ashamed, wondering whether they'd remember.

If it feels a tad Jayson Blair–esque that someone with a career based in telling the truth ran so fast and loose with it in her personal life, note that none of this lying extended to my reporting. (Or to this book, just FYI, and unfortunately for all my overburdened friends I have at least a decade's worth of Gchats to prove it.) If anything, one of the reasons I picked this industry was because the veracity it required offered some relief from my own struggle with it. Writing the truth for work opened up a pure space in my world, one where I could rest from trying to keep up with my lies.

Outside work, though, I claimed I'd been sleeping with a twenty-year-old Spanish man I'd invented out of thin air. He was very sexy. Another time, I alleged I'd had a lengthy romantic relationship with a friend of a friend, even though we'd kissed exactly one time before he ran away from me forever. He was less sexy. And I lied about mundane things, like whom I was out with the night before or who my friends were. These stories didn't come out of me often, but it happened enough that I feared I would never be able to stop. And if I never stopped, I would never truly be me.

•

I do not lie anymore. I'm sure that's hard to believe, since I just spent 1,500 words telling you I used to drop more falsehoods than Donald Trump does at one of his Special Very Good Big Boy Appreciation rallies. And yet it's true. One day I was a liar, and the next I was not. I haven't quite figured out how that happened, but somehow it did.

When I was twenty-five, I did start seeing a therapist. I went because I was depressed enough to make people worry about me, particularly the two people who birthed me and figured they'd somehow managed to screw me up. My therapist was a sharp-toned middle-aged woman who had an office in the West Village and always started our sessions about ten minutes late. I talked about a lot of things with her, like how I worried constantly that I was too short to love. She mostly asked me questions about my mother. And at some point, early on in our time together, I revealed to her my deepest shame.

"I'm a compulsive liar," I told her. "I used to lie all the time, and now I still lie sometimes, and I can't seem to stop doing it."

My therapist peered at me over the notepad on which I assumed she regularly spent forty-five minutes scribbling *INSTITUTIONALIZE THIS BITCH.*

"Let's talk about your mother," she said.

"But don't you want to discuss my lying?" I asked. "It's a really big problem!"

"I'd rather talk about your mother," my therapist said. Or maybe she didn't say quite that. I can't remember for sure, and I don't want to lie to you. Either way, we didn't discuss it, and we definitely did talk about my mother for the next fifty sessions.

At the time I didn't find all that focus on my mother helpful, yet four years later, I cannot remember when I last told a big lie. In fact, something perhaps more horrible happened to me—I became mostly *incapable* of telling lies. I have never had a good poker face, despite all my falsehoods, but in my subconscious quest to stop telling people I had a boyfriend in high school, I became a brutal truth teller, unable even to placate wounded friends with harmless white fibs. It turns out telling your buddy you think her boyfriend is ambulatory sludge isn't a good way to make that friend feel better about the fact that he called her fat, and that when people ask you, "How are you?" they don't expect you to divulge all your fears about a suspicious lump you found under your armpit or mention that you were too depressed to get out of bed last week. People no longer want to try on clothes near you. It's hard to break up with people when you have to tell them why (a good work-around is to just block them on your phone).

On the other hand, the more I told the truth, the less I suffered panic attacks over the possibility of being revealed as a fraud. And the more I became comfortable with existing in the world as myself—the more I told my truths, listened to other people's, and stopped treating bar nights like a Moth storytelling slam—the more I learned to enjoy the experiences I had, not the ones I made up. My friends did not abandon the real me, not even the aforementioned friend with the shithead boyfriend. Perhaps I used savage honesty as a way to repent, but in the end it did help cut out the root cause of my compulsions. I may not have learned to love myself (a task best left to psychopaths and people who like things made of hemp), but I was at the very least enough as I was.

In journalism, you tell Universal Truths and the Truths of others. In fiction, you attempt to tell the emotional truth in a false reality. In neither of these disciplines are you required to slice open your head and reveal the madness inside; in both, you are invited to manipulate the truth, to present it as you want it to be seen, and to smooth over the bits that don't fit if need be.

Serious writers sneer at personal essays all the time, and it's true that it takes a certain kind of narcissism to think your own shit is interesting. But essays do require the writer to present an unairbrushed version of themselves, one without journalism's veil of objectivity or fiction's innate Photoshop. I once took a class on creative nonfiction and wrote a story about learning to dive as a child. I concluded my piece with a scene in which I do a perfect swan dive, even though I have probably never done anything in water that did not resemble a hamster drowning. My instructor was not impressed with the self-celebration. "We are never the heroes of our own stories," he said. "People want to see you fail. It's funnier." He was right, though I'm not sure I agree with his reasoning. It's not so much that people want to laugh at you when you fail. Mostly, I think, since we're all failing all the time, someone else's failures make us feel better about our own.

I read a lot of stories with happy endings in my youth. The quirky weird girls still came out okay in the end, and no matter how hard I tried, I did not. But those quirky weird girls had adult writers gifting them hot boyfriends and clear skin—in part, I assume, because that was the story the adult writers had wanted for themselves but never got. It's not fancy to write an entire book about a girl who spends her spare time making the eyes of Sims characters bigger, but that's who I was. Sometimes I wonder what I might have been had I known it was normal to walk through the world feeling like I was made wrong.

Everyone lies. Compulsive liars do it blatantly and detest themselves more for it, but there isn't one idiot walking this earth who doesn't lie at least once every day, even if that lie is just answering the question "How are you?" with "Fine." We lie to our friends, we lie to our families, we lie to our employers, we lie to our lovers, we lie to our children, we lie on social media, and we lie all the fucking time in the mirror.

My grandfather once told me it was better to be nice than to be honest. I will never be nice. I will never be better. I will be good. Niceness only helps incubate the lies we tell ourselves and the ones we present to others. I choose the truth, even if the truth is selfish and stupid. It is better to be good than to be nice, even if "good" means showing all your warts and being okay with telling people you spent the night marathoning *Buffy the Vampire Slayer* instead of partying, that you ordered chicken on Seamless because you don't know how to cook it, that you didn't vote for Bernie Sanders, that you are scared of big dogs, that no boys wanted to kiss you in high school, and that you worry all the time that you are too unhinged and intense and demanding (and maybe too short, because therapy hasn't fixed that) to love. I will not lie to you about my warts, and I do not want you to lie to me about yours. If it is the truth, it's enough.

Sometimes Your Irrational Fears Come True and Fire Destroys Your Home

As a child with an overactive imagination, I was afraid of everything. I knew that everything on the planet was specifically designed to kill me, so I stayed away from high ledges and the monkey bars and sand. The world is a scary place for children who are aware of their own mortality, and my nights were haunted by visions of hidden dangers like car crashes, plane crashes, trees crashing into buildings, rabid dogs, and salmonella.

If my family left our apartment empty for the weekend, I envisioned returning to a pile of ash. There was always the possibility that someone forgot to unplug the toaster or blow out a candle or check the closets for a hidden pyromaniac just waiting for the chance to strike. If we were out together in the neighborhood, I'd hear fire truck sirens and expect them to meet us back at the barren pit where our building once stood. Fire-fighters would shrug and gesture at the rubble. My mother would blame me for leaving my bed unmade near an outlet.

To combat some of this pyrophobia, I made plans, should the need to evacuate ever arise. We practiced fire drills in school, collectively Stopping, Dropping, and Rolling in attempt to extinguish imaginary flames that had engulfed us, an exercise I also practiced at home, just in case. I would take with me, should a real fire happen, my favorite doll, Dollydoll, and the blanket I used as a pillow, named Pillow Blankie (my afore-mentioned imagination did not extend to naming comfort toys). I would make sure my parents and my sister were with me, as I'd need them later for cash and emotional support. We'd run down the side stairs and out of the building, into safety across the street. If somehow the flames caught up with me, I'd "stop, drop, and roll," per the aforementioned drills. Then when the fire was finally extinguished, I'd dig through what was left of my home, finding what few belongings had survived. Bad things were always around the corner. I just hadn't experienced them yet.

Fast-forward a decade or two. When I first moved back to New York after college, I lived in an apartment in Williamsburg that I loved but couldn't afford. After spending a year sobbing over each rent check, I decamped for a lofted room in Bushwick with a much lower rent but many more mouse infestations, bedbug scares, midnight experimental music jams, and nearby bars with unclear policies regarding outdoor noise. One year, I roomed with an actress who neglected to tell us she intended to move her boyfriend in with us about five seconds after signing the lease. Every night he'd come over at one A.M. so they could spend the next several hours loudly bickering with and/or sexy-biting each other right underneath me. They are now married! I wish them well.

In April 2015, I abandoned Bushwick and moved into an empty bedroom in my friend's apartment in Greenpoint. It was a charming little space, and though it hardly fit the two of us—indeed, the kitchen was so small the landlord had had to lop off half the counter to wedge the fridge in—it was the first place I'd lived in that felt like home. I had a real room, with a regular ceiling and walls that had yet to have bedbug-fighting poison drilled in. I had a living room with a television. I had a sunlit view of Manhattan Avenue. I had a $10-a-month gym next door and a yoga studio up the block. I had trees on my street. I did not have drunk NYU kids screaming outside my window at three A.M. on a weeknight. I was in heaven.

Six months into this utopia, my roommate, Emma, started dating someone, and it looked like it was going to turn serious. I was happy for her but also started considering my options. What if they wanted to move in together when our lease was up? What if she wanted to move anyway? What if she hated me? What if the rent went up? What if someone else moved in? I knew once I got too comfortable somewhere, something bad would come along and take it from me—after all, when things were good, there was only room for them to go bad. I had bounced around from one miserable living situation to another over the years, and I was too happy with this particular one to stomach the thought of living next-door to one more amateur jam band. Which meant, of course, that I was doomed.

I was particularly plagued by this concern on the night of October 19. I had just come from a glorious yoga session and was unwinding with a nice glass of Polish Christmas wine. Emma's boyfriend, with whom she usually stayed in his one-bed in Prospect Heights, was crashing with us because his landlord hadn't turned on his heat. I checked the listings in Greenpoint, *just in case,* then closed my computer and went to sleep. I dreamt of nothing.

I woke up to knocking. Emma's voice wafted into my room. "There's a fire," she said. "We have to go." I sensed a faint smell of smoke in my room and a definite haze. Siren lights blinked in through the window. I had been sleeping pants-less in a crop top, as was my fashion-forward custom, so I pulled a pair of crumpled leggings off my floor, stepped into an old pair of Top-Siders, and took my leather jacket, my phone, and my keys. In my sleep brain I assumed we'd be let back inside momentarily, but when Emma, her boyfriend, and I walked into the hall, I spotted smoke billowing out from under our neighbor's door. When we got outside, the first thing I saw were the fire trucks clustered around the building. The second thing I saw was the literal fire, which lit up the hardware store located almost directly beneath my bedroom. We were in for some shit.

The thing about watching disaster unfold is that you don't realize it's disaster while the shock is giving you a hug. You just keep watching. There's nothing else to do. We stood inside the deli across the street and watched the drama go down, though the madness seemed farther than just a few feet away. I drank a hot chocolate as the firefighters hooked a ladder to the building's facade, right under my window, then pulled my window out of its little home. I watched through the window socket as they flipped my bed over and climbed into my room. Briefly, I considered the mess their big firefighter boots would make on my floor, before I watched one pull out an axe and hack through one of my walls, à la Jack Nicholson in *The Shining*. "Our rent better not go up," I said, sipping my drink. Emma laughed.

The flames were still going strong in the hardware store, so it appeared we wouldn't be going home for the night, assuming we'd even have a home after this. Fire inspectors and representatives with the Office of Emergency Management took down our information while our neighbors filled us in on the parts of the night we'd missed. The drunk chick in "Suite #1" had come home late and smelled the smoke, so she'd awoken her roommates and everyone else in the building. God bless the drunk chick. Maybe she saved our lives—at the very least, she saved me from waking up to a firefighter chopping through my window, which would have taken more therapy to recover from than I could afford. As my neighbors spoke, I realized my leggings were inside out. I was still wearing my retainer. I am very responsible.

I texted a friend that my building was on fire, knowing he would come. He showed up with a coat. Emma and her boyfriend relocated to his apartment in Prospect Heights, promising to meet again in the morning to go through the wreckage. My friend took me to his apartment, where he gave me a blanket his mother made him and set me up on his couch. I listened to him breathe through the door of his room and wondered what would happen if I went in there and climbed into bed with him. I didn't know if that was what I wanted, but I didn't want to be alone on his couch and in my head.

My hair, skin, and clothes smelled like cedar and burnt plastic, a sickly-sweet smell of wood gone bad. In that moment, the only things in the world that I owned were my crop top, leggings, Top-Siders, and jacket. I kicked myself for leaving my wallet. I recalled an old yoga refrain, lay on my side, and felt the earth—er, couch—beneath me. At some point, I suppose, I slept. All of this happened within the span of a few hours. I was in shock until morning, and even when I woke up, smelled the burnt plastic—undeniable evidence of what had transpired—remembered where I was, and why I was there, I felt as if I were moving in someone else's body, watching myself lie on the couch from above.

I returned to my building to discover it was still standing, which was at first a relief. On closer look, I wasn't so lucky. Most of my belongings were ruined. My mattress was in the living room, where I assume it landed after the firefighters axed it. My roommate's collection of used VHS tapes lay shattered on the ground. The whole place was covered with a fine layer of ashen, toxic smoke that had made its way into almost everything I owned. The apartment and everything in it smelled like a campfire—not a comforting one, but one filled with tiny particles that would invade your blood cells and turn them against one another. The particles lived in my couch, in my bed, in my laptop, in my television, on my plates, and in every dress, shoe, T-shirt, and towel I owned. It was all poison.

As I'd oft envisioned in my childhood fire dreams, I gathered up my favorite things and threw them into plastic boxes Emma and her boyfriend procured, in hopes that the power of dry cleaning could save them. At the very least, I didn't want to leave the things I loved most behind in the noxious place I was about to abandon. I called a boy who'd broken my heart a few months prior and asked if he could drive me and my ash-covered combat boots up to my parents' place on the Upper West Side. He said yes. I made him buy me pizza. He got a parking ticket. For a moment, I was pleased.

·

A lot happened in the aftermath of that night. I had renters insurance, blessedly, so a few days after the fire I met with an insurance man, who came to the apartment to make sure it really had been destroyed. He looked around—not just at the hacked-up walls and soot-stained floors, but at our ratty couch and freestanding IKEA closets—and suggested throwing everything out. "All of it?" I said, thinking of the five drawers stuffed with clothing in my bedroom. "Do you . . . really want it?" he said, glancing at a mounted portrait of a man's torso with a bottle opener attached to his crotch. He had a point.

So I had to dump all my junk and hope I'd get enough fancy insurance money to buy new junk. This required me to spend several hours combing through each piece of clothing in my wardrobe to decide which of my beloved $50 Urban Outfitters dresses were worth dry cleaning. Turns out, none of them were, and they all went in the trash.

A week later, my apartment still smelled like burnt plastic and was deemed unlivable by the Department of Buildings, so I moved in with my parents. Now Brooklyn and my old life seemed really far away (at *least* a forty-minute train ride, with transfers!), and I spent intermittent days of the week crashing on people's couches and in their unoccupied beds. My sister had just graduated from college and was also living at home, which meant the two of us were back in our childhood bedroom fighting over who got to use the bathroom first in the morning. Most of my clothes were toast, so I ended up wearing a lot of relics from high school, like Chuck Taylor slip-ons and a pair of 7 for All Mankind jeans on which I once blew all my babysitting money. I had a curfew. I had to make my bed, which naturally was an extra-narrow twin. I shared it with a dozen or so stuffed bears, all of which had their own distinct personalities and complex familial backgrounds.

On the other hand, I was surrounded by people I loved and who loved me, who tended to make me dinner and let me fill up their DVR with reruns of *The Nanny*. It was a nice time, but it was also a weird time. I was lucky to have somewhere to crash while I waited for the insurance check to come through, but it was strange to abandon the life I'd worked so hard to make for myself so quickly. When I come home for short visits, I tend to turn into the person I was before I left for good, when I was seventeen and about to start college and become a new me. This time I wasn't sure when I'd be able to leave again, or where I'd go. For the most part, the things I had amassed over my years of independence, the totems and proof that I'd once had a room and an address and a life of my own, were gone. Incidentally, the things I'd once feared losing—my dolls, my toys, my Wayside School storybook collection—were pretty much the only things I had left.

•

The thing about losing most of your stuff is that stuff is just stuff. Before toxic smoke penetrated everything I owned, I cared a lot about getting new things. I was never a shopper per se, but buying new things was a form of self-care. Capitalism had taught me that I would feel better if I had a new T-shirt, and sometimes it did make me feel better. Other times I just had one more T-shirt. But there was security in having the things. I liked that they were safe with me in my apartment. I liked that the things that belonged to me slept near me in a drawer. We insulated each other from the outside world, heightening the difference all domesticated creatures assert—that there in fact *is* a difference between in here and out there.

Everything I owned, up to the fire, marked a specific point in time. I had dozens of chiffon shirts I'd gotten for free when I worked at a clothing store that I refused to throw out, just in case. I had hundreds of dollars' worth of nail polish that I bought during a particularly dark phase when I was on Weight Watchers and would go to Duane Reade to avoid drunk-eating. I had a hard drive full of photos from college, concert flyers I'd stolen from bars in Europe, a painting my grandmother made for me. All my books were gone. I loved all those things because they were mine, and now they were in a sanitation lot in Brooklyn. But it was just stuff.

I also lost a place. Though I still had somewhere to live, getting ejected from my little Greenpoint haven was like being thrown into a river. I missed my blue kitchen and my yoga studio and my Polish grocery store. I missed my commute. I missed being a person with her own address. I didn't miss paying rent, and my short reprieve at my childhood home meant I could stress less about having to replace all my belongings (the insurance check eventually did arrive, taking the edge off even more). Still, my little life in my little neighborhood had ended.

There's a phenomenon called *posttraumatic growth,* which researchers Richard Tedeschi and Lawrence Calhoun define as a "positive psychological change experienced as a result of adversity and other challenges in order to rise to a higher level of functioning." Basically, when something bad happens to you and you stare it down, you develop more confidence and the sense that you can face adversity, should it come your way again. I read about posttraumatic growth years after the fire when Hurricane Maria pummeled Puerto Rico, and though my small plight was far, far cushier than the unmitigated destruction and governmental abandonment of an entire island, something very odd did happen to me after I lost my things and my home. I knew I could survive a bad thing, and if that was the case, I could probably survive many more bad things, maybe even worse things, but certainly things that were decidedly less bad.

Back in my paranoid youth, disasters like fire, death, and monkey bar accidents were out of my control. That fear of not being in control extended into adulthood, even if I wasn't gripped with terror each night over potential catastrophe. Instead, I feared constantly that a boy I liked would drop me, or that I'd be trapped on a subway train overnight, or that I'd be fired and lose my income and my entire sense of self. But you can't really protect your parents from dying in a car crash, just as you can't stop electrical wiring in your illegally zoned Greenpoint apartment building from sparking in the middle of the night. You can't stop someone you care about from deciding not to care about you. Sometimes you lose your job. Sometimes you lose your home.

•

Of course, though I'd like to say the fire turned me into a minimalist, I now own fourteen pairs of jeans. Papers and sweaters and dust and errant hair ties and memories of bad decisions have piled up in every corner of my room in Brooklyn, which is now three years old but was new when I escaped into it several months after the fire. I shed my old shit just to get new shit, and though my new shit fits me better, I'm still weighed down by it all the time. Experiences change you in small ways, but you're never really fixed.

And in some ways, you're even more broken. Once, in my new apartment, the smoke detector went off in the middle of the night. I made my roommates march out of the apartment and stand across the street while we called the fire department. They cleared us to go back in, and I spent the rest of the night seeing phantom clouds dance across the room. It was nice to be safe, I suppose. But then again, the insurance money was nice, too.

Beauty Is in the Eye of the Beholder Except When the Teens Think You're a Hideous Beast

The internet is great for a lot of things, like googling photos of young Harrison Ford or looking up specific character traits for some of the rarer Muppets. There are times, though, in which the collective voice of the internet turns against you, transforming the World Wide Web from an encyclopedia ripe for near-anonymous browsing into a big pitchfork that angry Twitter townspeople can use to rip out your intestines. And few mob's tines are sharper than the ones wielded by Taylor Swift fans.

I was an OG Taylor Swift fan—which is to say, I myself loved her as an actual teen. I remember Taylor when her hair was curly, her voice twangy, and her songs imagined ballads about truck-driving boyfriends intent on proposing to her before she graduated from high school. A friend introduced me to Taylor Swift during my freshman year of college not long after she'd released her debut album, and though I wore a lot of scarves during that period, I *fucking* loved Taylor Swift. My sophomore year, "Forever & Always" came out right around the time a boy I occasionally made out with decided he didn't like me anymore, and I listened to it on repeat while I waited for him to text me back, which he never did. "'Was I OUT OF LINE?'" I'd scream along with Taylor in my room. "'Did I say something WAY TOO HONEST, made you RUN AND HIDE? / LIKE A SCARED LITTLE BOY?' HUH, SAM? DID I?" The rage didn't make him like me, but it was cathartic nonetheless.

I followed Taylor through college and into my early postgrad years. I have fond memories of making my sales associates listen to "We Are Never Ever Getting Back Together" while closing out the clothing store I floor-managed my first year out of school. When *1989* came out I wanted to hate it—I was twenty-five and too old and cool for Taylor Swift by then, you see—but I listened to "Blank Space" every single day on my walk to the train in Bushwick and thought about my own long list of ex-lovers who were probably telling people I was insane.

Taylor Swift's star started to decline with my people

when pop music, like everything else in the universe, became politicized by the 2016 election. By the time *Reputation* came out in 2017, she had become almost synonymous with mediocre white women who let the country fall to Trump. (I was a mediocre white woman who voted for Hillary, thank you very much.) Still, I accepted that Taylor Swift was my problematic fave. So you understand why it was a bit of a shock when the Taylor Swift fans came for me.

The Swifties Incident, as I like to call it, was a snowball. I was a recent entrant into the freelance workforce, and I'd picked up a couple blogging shifts with a very popular women's website. I was a fan of the site and very excited to work for them when someone asked me to cover their night shift. The catch was that I already had a day shift for a different site in the morning, and another one the *next* morning, so I was going to have to work nine A.M. to three P.M., then six P.M. to one A.M., then again from nine A.M. to three P.M. That's a lot of writing, especially considering that night shift would have me running a website I didn't know that well without anyone else online to catch my errors. But I was hungry for work and worried about being hungry in general, and you don't turn down jobs when you're new to the freelance grind, so I took it on.

The hardest thing about blogging for a website that's new to you is finding what to write about. When I worked at my local blog, we had a Google doc of story ideas, plus I knew the site so well I could find something appropriate in under ten minutes if I needed to. In New York, subway perverts abound in a pinch, after all. But with this beat, I still wasn't totally sure what would qualify as a story, and I was scared I'd screw up and endanger our budding relationship. (It turns out this fear was unfounded, as I once published a blog post titled "Reese Witherspoon Cleaned Her Own Hollywood Star, But Will She Come Clean My Room?" and continued to work. But that is neither here nor there.)

Long story short, in need of a story, I noticed Taylor Swift had said something stupid online, and I was good at writing about Taylor Swift. So I made a blog.

The blog, titled "Shut Up Taylor Swift, Everybody Hated 2017," called Swift out on a comment she made on her Instagram about having "the best year." For review, 2017 was a total fucking trash fire in which literal Nazis held rallies. Swift hadn't denounced the white nationalists who celebrated her for being an Aryan pop star, and was now saying the year that blessed us with these monsters was "the best." The blog was dumb, I wrote it in fifteen minutes, and I sent it out onto the internet. The backlash came quickly.

It's a specific kind of torture when a teen who hates you gets ahold of your Instagram. I learned this the hard way, when the following day I started getting photo comments and messages from handles like @taylor swiftfan1989 and @reputaytionforqueen excoriating me for daring to come for their girl. "I'm sorry but by writing this article you just showed that your belonged to those sad journalists/bloggers who do nothing but acting," one person posted. "Blogger aka someone with barely 500 followers ready to tear down successful artists just because her own year wasn't good," another wrote.

I have *550* Instagram followers, thank you very much, so I brushed it off. But when I woke up the next morning, the angry Swifty Instagram comments and mean tweets had multiplied. Most of them were about how much I sucked, how cruel I was for attacking a millionaire celebrity who would never hear of me, how I'd surely torn out sweet Taylor's heart by implying she should have had a bad year just because I did.

A bunch of celebrity stans calling me stupid and cruel didn't really faze me, as I am not stupid and I know for a fact that I am cruel. Still, as I recall from my own time as a teen, teens always know just the right place to stick the dagger, and some of the enraged Swifties were quick to find my soft spot. The most recent photo on my 'gram at the time of the Swiftening was a makeup-less selfie I took while bored—one I figured maybe fifteen people would see and/or care about, and maybe a guy I liked would think was cute—and the Swifties were quick to inform me that I was nowhere near as beautiful as their queen. In fact, they pointed out, I was *ugly.*

"The most ugly person I have ever seen, body and soul," one poster wrote. Another: "If I had a face like yours I'd have a bad year too, why don't you put on some makeup or some shit." One dug a little deeper into my Instagram feed, posting "ugly" on photos of me at a wedding, holding a winter squash, hugging my friends. On a photo of a friend's cat, they even posted "ugly cat."

Trolls love to call women ugly online. In a world in which appearance is still paramount for the once-deemed fairer sex, being ugly is a curse, a surefire sign that you're an Undesirable destined for a lonely future and a silent death at the paws of your many unkempt felines. Some women are able to brush off an attack on their physical appearances, having moved on, post-puberty, from the terror of discovering one of their eyes is slightly smaller than the other. Other women don't even have to contend with a slight against their looks, either because they're confident enough not to care or because they're so fucking hot no one would dare call them ugly in the first place.

I am not one of those women. My phone is full of selfies I have taken, not to marvel at my appearance, but to find each teeny flaw. I am very familiar with the awkward way my nose hooks over my nostrils, and the little extra flap of skin under my chin where stitches melted, thanks to an unfortunate seesaw incident. My teeth are crooked. My eyes are small. One of my eyebrows does not have as much hair as the other eyebrow. I am a monster.

I am not actually a monster. Most people are not actually ugly, just as most people are not actually beautiful. Some people have qualities that make them attractive to some people and not to others. Imperfections are interesting. Taylor Swift's eyes are also small. But the flood of strangers calling me ugly stuck right into the section of my brain that screams every time I go shopping for jeans, or maybe so much interaction with Taylor fans was regressing me to the Taylor-loving, self-hating teen I'd once been. I texted everyone I knew. "Am I ugly?" I begged them. "You would tell me if I were ugly, right?" (Certainly they would not.)

In the twenty-four hours following the Taylor Swift Attack, I devolved into madness. I looked through all my Facebook and Instagram photos at least twice. I took more selfies. I texted more friends. I journaled. I googled, "How do you know you are ugly?" and read a number of Reddit posts that varied in usefulness.

The belief that you are ugly embeds itself early. When I was six or seven, my aunt told me that if I picked my nose it would grow to be bulbous and big. "Like mine," she said, pointing to the monster gourd that sat atop her face. She scared me—not enough to stop me from digging up there, of course, as I am only human, but enough so I spent the next twenty years obsessing over the size and shape of my own increasingly protrusive organ. Indeed, I ended up with my aunt's nose, not because of the nose-picking, but because we share genes. BUT STILL.

At one point in my youth, my mother told me short women live difficult lives. "It's easier to be over five-two," she said, and so I spent my formative years regarding with pity the teachers, mothers, and other adults who didn't quite hit that target. I waited for the moment in which I would shoot up and stand above them on the pedestal reserved exclusively for the beautiful and tall, for when I would be willowy and beloved like Belle from *Beauty and the Beast,* whom I assumed, for some reason, that I'd resemble, even though I was blond and curly-haired and she was a literal drawing. But my growth spurt never came, and soon the classmates who'd stood in front of me when we lined up for school photos moved behind. When I was in fifth grade, my Snoopy-tie-clad pediatrician told me I was probably done growing. "You'll always be small," he said, writing *4'11* in his notes, and I screamed and kicked the examining table with my dumb little stubby legs that would never be long enough. I would never be five-two. I had failed. As punishment, my life would always be hard.

The summer before I started sixth grade, I spent my

first summer at sleepaway camp. I was short, chubby, and newly pubescent and harbored an obsession with Michael J. Fox that was rather outdated in 2000. One night we had a "social" with the boys' camp across the way. I dressed up in case someone resembled my beloved MJF, donning a tank top that showed off my arm fat and my friend's horseshit-caked riding boots that I thought were sexy. The girls looked me up and down. "Is that what you're wearing?" one asked. It was. "Have you looked at your hair?" I had not. They laughed at me. None of the boys at the social talked to me. I started to understand.

When I was sixteen, I found out a friend of mine was calling me ugly behind my back, and I never got over it. When I was in college, someone posted in my university's anonymous student message board that I was "ugly and bowlegged." I have still not gotten over it. (I may also be bowlegged? /shrug.) No matter how many men have told me I am beautiful in order to trick me into having sex with them, I do not believe it. When they dump me, I know it's because they noticed that my nose looks like a potato in the right light. If I dump them, it's because you can't trust someone who likes an ugly girl, and also maybe because they laughed weird.

It did not escape me, when the Swifties came for me, that the person I wanted to look like, back when I was young and dreamed of growing up beautiful, was

Taylor Swift. Not specifically her, of course, but the paragon of womanly Westernized beauty—tall, thin, long-legged, with bouncy smooth hair and big red lips, just like Taylor. This perception of beauty is starting to shift. Models, actors, and singers do not need to be white-skinned and thin-nosed and European-esque to be considered beautiful. But the shift hadn't quite made it to me as a child in the 1990s, and it hasn't pervaded society enough at this point that people don't think someone that looks like Taylor Swift exemplifies True Beauty, a fact made clear to me by the Swifties.

"I would hate Taylor Swift too, if I looked like Rebecca Fishbein," one fan tweeted at me, and maybe he's right. Maybe I tried to cut down a celebrity because I wish I looked like her and owned her house and drove her car. Maybe it was just my job to make a blog, and it was ten P.M., and I was very tired. Either way, I had questioned the human paragon of beauty. Therefore I was "ugly," because who was I, with my big Jew nose and wild hair and slightly unfilled left eyebrow, to fight the rules governing good looks? Beautiful women are untouchable. If you are not one of them, if you question them, armies of people will literally rise up to tell you why you're too hideous to speak their name.

In the midst of the attack of the Swifties, after the four hundredth person messaged me to inform me that I should be more supportive of women, *you cunt,* my roommate asked me how I handled the trolls. "I ignore them," I offered. This is usually true, but not always, which I imagine is the same answer celebrities give when people ask how they feel about the tabloids running headlines on their five-pound weight gain. I'm sure someone has called Taylor Swift ugly and made her cry, based on the many sad songs she's put out (although if they did it publicly, I can only assume the fans had them assassinated).

The thing about thinking you're ugly is that at some point you learn to live with the self-hatred. When I was in college, there was a 0 percent chance I'd leave my dorm room without applying approximately eight layers of mascara, for fear that someone would spot my blond eyelashes and mistake me for an extraterrestrial. Last week I went to the grocery store—not the one across the street from my apartment, but the one *three whole avenues away*—wearing torn leggings I'd slept in, no bra, an inside-out crop top, and a part of a face mask. What happened between then and now? Laziness, mostly, but also I got tired of looking in the mirror and seeing nothing but a collage of my flaws. So I chose not to look, or rather, I chose not to *care* the way I used to.

You can't change your face, at least not without some serious cash, and for the unhappiest of us, even that probably won't make you like yourself much better.

Studies show people who have rhinoplasty often regret messing with their faces. There are so many more things to worry about than a big nose and gaping pores—impending nuclear war, a growing economic divide, whether or not my upstairs neighbors' space heater will kill me in my sleep—and in the end, our faces all turn into waxlike accordions and our bodies into useless bags of atrophied muscle and crumbling bone. If we're lucky! We're all going to die. There's only so much time to fixate.

Eventually the Swiftian terror stopped. The teens moved on to attack some other unsuspecting journalist who dared say something derisive about Taylor ALISON Swift, an ICON. I made my Instagram account private and spent less time, but still too much time, looking in the mirror. Mostly I forgot about the flame-throwing fans and limited meltdowns over my physical appearance to the aforementioned jeans-shopping. Still, I kept the Reddit threads and YouTube videos on contouring bookmarked, just in case I accidentally said something mean in the future about Lana Del Rey, and the word *ugly* is alive somewhere in my brain.

Never doubt the power of a fan.

The Definition of Insanity Is Doing the Same Thing Over and Over Again and Expecting Different Results, but Why Not Give It One More Try?

A thing normal people know that I have never learned is that you should not shit where you eat. This is common wisdom, a warning repeated every time someone mentions a coworker or boss or roommate or best friend or best friend's boyfriend or barista at the good coffee shop with that little pitch in their voice that indicates they want to fuck that person's brains out. "Don't shit where you eat!" the wise friend tells the starry-eyed idiot fully intent on upending their life. "Don't foul your own nest! Don't dip your pen in the company ink! Don't shoot holes in your own boat! Don't get your meat at the same place you get your bread!"

Hopefully, the horny fool takes that adage soup to heart and finds some available person to make babies with instead. But *I* will never listen, and will in fact insist on shitting all over my kitchen and everybody else's kitchen until *E. coli* ravages my intestines and turns my human body into a listless pile of bloody diarrhea. Which, of course, I'll also leave in the kitchen, where I eat.

I don't know where I developed a habit of fucking all my friends. The self-help books I read in the stacks at the Strand say sexual perversions start to develop before the age of two, which is distressing for a bunch of reasons. Perhaps my brain wildly misinterpreted all the lessons George Carlin imparted on *Shining Time Station*, or maybe I picked up on Bert and Ernie's special vibes, who knows. Whatever the root cause, if you are a man I spend a lot of time with—in my home, at my place of work, in my close and intimate group of friends—at some point I will probably sleep with and subsequently hate you.

The film opens the same way each time. I have an innocuous platonic relationship with someone in close proximity to me, and I rarely, if ever, think about them or acknowledge they have a penis I might like to meet. But time passes, our banter picks up a comfortable rhythm, I drink with them too late one night, and all of a sudden that mole I thought looked gross starts to seem sexy. They look at me too long for just a moment, tuck my hair behind my ears, maybe put a steadying hand on my back, say something like, "Are you okay? Do you need me to get you an Uber? Please don't take another shot," and that's it. I'm hooked.

Not that I tell them I'm hooked, of course. First there is a period of infatuation. In this period, I pick over every single one of our interactions, looking for small moments that either prove to me my new object of affection is into it or reassure me that I am a disgusting trash person and this individual would much prefer to bone my best friend. I spend late nights studying his Facebook photos and his ex-girlfriends' Facebook photos, google-mapping his childhood homes, and reading about how his third cousin twice removed saved a baby whale from certain death in the summer of 1986 in the archives of his hometown paper.

I detail every conversation he and I have to each of the friends I do not (in that moment) want to fuck. "Do you think he likes me?" I say as I present them with swaths of Gchat messages for analysis, presumably to their utter delight. I then fight them when they offer words of encouragement and refuse to talk to them if they give me bad news. And I think about this person constantly, keeping him in a corner of my brain at all times, carrying him with me when I walk down the street or go for a run or cry in the shower as I envision the moment in which he finally tells me he thinks I'm ugly.

These infatuations can last for any period of time. Once I crushed hard on an editor after he took me out for drinks at a fancy rooftop bar, only to have it dissipate fully after two weeks of stalking his Flickr photos from 2005. Another time I spent a night unleashing the full power of my secret obsessive passion on the Instagram account of a close friend, and had forgotten about it when I awoke the next morning. And on one occasion I decided the manager at the clothing store I worked at was my soulmate and plotted to change my schedule to match his, only to discover about a month later that he was secretly sleeping with no fewer than four other employees, which was at least one too many for me to compete with.

These were brief fixations and yielded no results, a blessing in the case of my editor, and also probably my manager, if only for the sake of my vaginal health. I forgot about two out of the three mentioned above until I started writing this very essay. But if I let this infatuation period run too long, it consumes me, which is especially true if I find myself in close proximity to the object of my obsession on a regular basis, where there's little room for distraction. Then these preoccupations have a habit of turning into intense ordeals that build up and up and up before ultimately deflating like a very sad balloon at a fair. A Sex Faire, if you will, but with no turkey legs, and in some particularly depressing cases, no sex at all.

The most miserable of these was the ten-month period of silent yearning I afforded a coworker. Some of that is detailed elsewhere in this book, but for theme's sake, the crucial detail is that he sat across from me in our small communal open office, and I could not escape him and thus an attraction bloomed over time. When I first met him, I hated him—I thought he was obnoxious, annoying, and a perfect example of a Mediocre White Man. I dreaded having to work with him. It took several years of close regular contact and shared snarky blog posts for me to start sensing that all that head-butting made him feel like home, and that I had been waiting all this time for this, to find someone whose brain and face and nerve endings fit mine.

There were some conflicting issues with our long-term goals, since he wanted to have sex with me so we could "get it out of our system" (his words), and I wanted to marry him and birth up to three of his children. At which point sitting across from him all day every day went from being a dream to a daily terror.

You'd think that experience would have been enough to turn me off on taking craps all over the cafeteria, but I am not a smart person. Not long after my coworker fed my main artery to the wolves, I decided to pursue a freelancer friend who had helped counsel me through my miserable dumb heartbreak. In fairness, this dude was hard to read. He made me dinner a few times, told me I was pretty, and showed up to my apartment with flowers one day when I was sick. "I'm the Joe Fox to your Kathleen Kelly!" he proclaimed, daisies in hand. One can only assume anyone referencing classic rom-com material like *You've Got Mail* wants to bone, so I made a move.

He did want to bone, it turns out, but not enough to want to keep boning, so he dropped me, too, informing me over Gchat that he'd rather just be friends so he could fuck other women and not me. Shortly thereafter, at a beloved colleague's going-away party, my boss announced she'd hired said freelancer as the replacement. I burst into tears. He took up real estate in my office a few weeks later, just a few desks away from nightmare coworker number one, and I suffered yet another year's worth of workplace misery.

Surely by now a well-adjusted individual would seek out a nice Tinder stranger to marry, instead of digging her claws into yet another person who is located just feet away from her at all times. But as I have already pointed out, I am not smart, and I am nowhere near well adjusted. Having laid waste to my workplace like the ambulatory HR violation I am, I set my stupid sights on the next closest possible location: my apartment.

After my beloved Greenpoint apartment caught fire and thrust me into the pit of hell that is room-hunting in Brooklyn, I moved into a place near Prospect Park with two roommates. Unfortunately, one of these roommates happened to be a man, and it appears that for me men are like bags of chips—if you keep them in the house, I'll eventually end up craving them and drunkenly shoving them into my mouth. When I met him, he was impeccably dressed, lived with two women, and worked for a fashion company, so I assumed he was gay and therefore safe from my maelstrom of thirst. He was neither of those things, it turned out. The day after I moved in, he fished a paper towel roll off a high shelf for me, and soon he hopped right into my love-and-sex-starved little head. I got stuck on him, wincing when he mentioned women he liked, blushing when I ran into him on the way to the shower before retreating to my room alone to marathon *New Girl* with my headphones plugged in so he wouldn't suspect.

It turns out secretly lusting after your roommate is rather fun. As is true with having a work crush, daily interactions mean daily dopamine spikes, and in this case, there were quite a few of them. One time I came home sad after work to find my roommate on our couch watching music videos; to cheer me up, he put on bands that I liked, and we drank beer and did karaoke until late into the night. Another time, I came home and threw up on my bedroom floor, and he fed me water and watched *Silicon Valley* with me until I felt well enough to go to bed. It was nice to be given attention so regularly, and it made me less compelled to go out and find a stranger to fill me up instead.

But like all relationships built on proximity and convenience rather than communication and compatibility, once things got real, they got fucked. We made out one bourbon-filled summer evening, and we started sleeping together that fall, against the counsel of literally every human I have ever met and/or cornered in a bar. We watched movies together, made dinner, and talked about the future, but never *our* future, which lived somewhere behind an iron curtain neither one of us attempted to breach. And then, as the Wise Friends forewarned, one day that winter he came home and announced he had met someone else. I was trapped for months with him in the room next to me, waiting for his light to turn on when he came in late at night, or not to turn on at all.

These were three big nightmares of my own making, but there've been others along the way—college friends, journalist friends, friends of friends, friends' siblings, coworkers, coworkers' siblings, interns—that I've pinged on or slept with or made out with in the dark on a crowded dance floor, leaving a trail of havoc in my wake. I am roasted on the regular for these exploits. I am routinely punished. I have been uninvited from parties, left out of group hangs, and ejected from some social circles altogether. But I'm also under the impression that this wasn't always such a gasp-worthy fetish. Once upon a time, it was normal to click with the people you met in the wild and loved most. There was a period in history in which folks married their high school sweethearts, secretaries, bosses, neighbors, third cousins, very best friends. Never forget that Sally wifed up with Harry in the end.

But in 2018, we date online strangers to avoid the kinds of complications that come with fucking someone you know. With a stranger, your lives are not yet intertwined, and so there are no real feelings to hurt or friendships to irrevocably ruin. If you don't like someone, you never have to see or hear from them again, and there's a whole cadre of other anonymous men and their skydiving photos to dig into whenever you need someone new. When you hop into bed with a stranger, you aren't required to follow up. When they sleep with other people, you don't overhear them bragging about it in the office kitchen. When someone ghosts you after a couple of dates, they don't even know you yet. They can't possibly be rejecting you for all the reasons you already know they should.

For me, though, proximity is a drug. The closer you

are to me, the more time I have to decide all the little things about you that I hate are actually worthy of my admiration. Like Jason Alexander in the World's Worst Film™ *Shallow Hal*, I see everyone else's flaws as a reflection of my own. If your eyes are too close together or your hands are too small or you say "between you and I" or have bad taste in bagels, I see in you my small eyes, short legs, buckteeth, frizzy hair, communication issues, fear of commitment, fear of airplanes, fear of mice, loud voice, dumb accent, bad opinions, bad taste in music, bad habits, general impatience, untidiness, laziness, picky eating, overeating, overdrinking, lack of interest in international politics, reluctance to take criticism, reluctance to take edits, general narcissism, and all-around horrendous personality.

I've heard many women say they've turned inadequate men down because they deserve the best, but I *know* I deserve the worst. And so when I meet a stranger who embodies even the slightest faults, I'm quick to assume all my defects are catching up to me. I don't make an effort to see the good in any of my Tinder dates, because to do so would require me to go on more dates, and I'm already convinced your speech impediment is punishment for my stupid lisp. I don't need you to make me hate myself more than I already do.

But if I know you, there's plenty of time, in my pining for you from afar, to transform your improprieties into beacons of attraction. When you're stuck in my face all day, when you live permanently in the far reaches of my peripheral vision, your compulsions become cute and your blemishes a turn-on. Since you didn't enter my life as a potential suitor, the pressure's off; instead of fearing you like me only because you are as worthless as I am, I have the chance to win you over, which will prove to you and myself that despite all my foibles, there's something in me that's good enough to warrant your time and affection.

And then of course, there's this: if you have decided to befriend me, have suffered through my bad takes and bad habits and still choose me, then I have nothing left to hide from you. I am able to believe that you like me for who I am, despite the bad things or perhaps even because of them. There is a risk with the strangers, flawed or otherwise, that the minute I fall for them they'll see through me, hate me, torture and leave me. My friends know I'm contrarian and always late; they know I refuse to eat vegetables and bring my own bread to dinner parties, that I have no core muscles and that one of my eyes gets lazy when tired. They know I demand too much from other people and not enough from myself, and yet they still stick around.

Ergo, when I conceptualize sleeping with a friend, I don't fear they'll dispose of me the second I reveal all my dark spots, which makes it easier to take the plunge.

Of course, this changes when I actually do jump in, since it turns out people can care for you and still not choose you. No matter how many of these platonic-turned-not friends *tell* me they think about me constantly, they adore me, they'd jump in front of a car to save me, when I ask them to *show* me, they're out. And then I'm forced to reckon with this: perhaps even the people who love me most will never love me enough, and it will always be this way.

Still, I keep trying—to date strangers, to date my friends, to date my friends' friends, to sit alone in my apartment and think about dating the dude with the cute dog I bumped into on the staircase—just in case. Maybe I will once again take a dump in my dining room, but do so in *just* the right corner of the trough that I'll manage to spare myself the intestinal bacteria this time. To be fair, it hasn't killed me yet.

Friends Stick with You Through Thick and Thin, Unless You Have Bedbugs

The other night, an acquaintance of mine threw a surprise party for her boyfriend. I had a bad cold and had just gotten back from an out-of-town weekend where I spent too much money, so I figured I'd go for a drink, give them a hug, and head home. But my hot friend's hot twin brother showed up and announced he was "maybe" breaking up with his live-in girlfriend, so I drank four Fernet and Cokes and tried to make out with him. Then I went home and went to sleep, and when I woke up at two A.M., I got out of bed and threw up on the floor.

I have thrown up on many a floor in my day, including that very floor at least once, and so none of this story is remarkable, save for one very important fact: I wasn't alone in my room. Was I with the hot almost-single twin? LOL, *nope*. There, blinking at me from a fold in my cotton pillowcase, was a tiny brown bedbug swelled with blood. That motherfucker had just bitten me, it was watching me clean up my stomach refuse in shame, and it was going to temporarily ruin my life. "FUCK YOU, LITTLE BUG!" I screamed as I squashed it dead, but that wasn't nearly enough revenge for what was to come.

If you've never had a bedbug infestation or seen a bedbug or espied a bedbug on your pillow judging you for sullying its home with your vomit, let me assure you: bedbugs are exactly the nightmare everyone describes. Stories about unending infestations, evil little bites that leave dark marks on your body, and nights spent trying to cram every goddamn stupid piece of clothing you own into the dryer before the laundromat closes do not exist just to sell you mattress encasements. Bedbugs are real, and they are the harbingers of physical and mental destruction, a fact I can attest to because my sweet, sweet blood and I are to bedbugs what an overripe afternoon fruit basket is to a swarm of fruit flies.

I have suffered no fewer than four bedbug infestations in the past ten years, mostly very minor, all harrowing. I got bedbugs for the first time in my very first adult apartment in New York, a beautiful, crumbling little thing located next door to a pastrami factory in Williamsburg. My room at the time consisted mainly of a bed and an impenetrable pile of clothes surrounding it, and the bugs decided to transform that clothing pile into a luxury nest. My roommate and I were moving out in two weeks at the time of the attack, so we spent our remaining tenancy lugging trash bags full of our belongings to the laundromat, hoping to spot errant quarters on the walk over. I didn't actually see any insects during that particular escapade, so to me they seemed like invisible little mites that nibbled at my skin whenever I was still. I sensed them everywhere, even after we were out of our infested apartment and in a new, hopefully less infested one in Bushwick.

Six months later, on Valentine's Day, I was in my little Bushwick attic room with the bottle of Two-Buck Chuck I'd elected to spend the night with, when I decided, for some reason, to take a peek behind my bed. There, wedged between my mattress and the wall, was a rather terrifying beetle-like thing the size of an apple seed. My first round in the bedbug ring turned me into a bedbug expert, thanks to the many, many, many, many, many, many, many, many sleepless hours I spent researching the sleeping/eating/pooping/mating/migrating/Netflix-bingeing habits of these terrible little beasts, so I recognized my enemy in an instant.

I informed my roommates, both of whom had boyfriends to spend Valentine's Day with instead of a bottle of mutant dead bird wine and a bedbug. They told me they were unconvinced we were infested. I was too afraid of them to argue, so I relinquished several hundred dollars I had genuinely intended to give the government to an exterminator to zap the ever-loving fuck out of the critters living in my abode. A fun fact about anxiety is that it gets eighty times worse when you really do have something to be anxious about, and tiny bugs taking over your bed and brain is definitively an anxiety-inducing event. I am also very good at tricking myself into believing I have diseases and weird rashes. I became convinced every tiny red mark on my body was a by-product of bug snack time, and I kept my exterminator, a handsome man named Stephen, coming back for longer than the requisite three treatments.

Indeed, on a biweekly basis, my new friend would spray his beautiful murder serum all over my floor and tell me how many dead bugs he found (total count in three months: one). I spent so much time with him I considered sending him sexy photos—dust balls, crumbs, a couple carpet beetles, an old fingernail, and other stuff that got me excited in the night. We didn't find any more bugs, despite the persistent appearance of red marks on my torso, and so eventually my beloved bug wrangler, likely exhausted by my daily emails, drilled poison holes in my walls, hopped in a van, and drove out of my life forever. I still saw random red marks and I REMAIN UNCONVINCED of the mission's success, but two months after Stephen departed, I stopped dreaming about bugs, and that was good enough for me.

And thus I entered a multiyear period of blissful bedbuglessness. Not that the little fuckers hadn't left their mark on my psyche. Bedbugs infest your brain far worse than they do your living quarters, and you see them everywhere eons after they're gone. And so, in my respite from bedbuggery, I still threw every thrift store purchase in the dryer before letting it cross my threshold. I inspected every single mosquito bite and hive rash. I checked my mattress for telltale bloodstains and fecal matter. A roommate once brought home a wooden shelf she found on the street and I considered calling the police.

Travel was the stuff of horror. The same year I suffered the second unending "infestation," I went on a three-week backpacking trip through Europe. I'd been pro-hostel on previous trips, but now that I was scarred by bugs, I imagined tiny Euro-parasites crawling on my skin, into my bag, and onto the plane headed back to my American bed.

Still, all stayed silent on the bedbug front. Then one August a new roommate moved into my apartment, inadvertently bringing with her a few dozen more new, decidedly less welcome roommates. The infestation was limited to her room, but the exterminators our landlord chose made all three of us living in the apartment run every goddamn piece of clothing we owned through a dryer, an exhausting, time-consuming task that cost me a surprising amount of money and a couple good dresses. And once again I was left feeling violated, though at least I was comforted that MY bed was safe. OR SO I THOUGHT.

Context for this particular pillowcase bug spotting: I hadn't had sex in five months, I was regularly bleeding money, and I finished all the seasons of *The Great British Bake Off* available on Netflix at that time, so things were not going well. Did I have time to heat all my shit up? Did I have the brain space to lie awake and imagine tiny beetles nibbling at my flesh? Did I have the energy to fear leaving bug bodies in my wake every time I walked into the living room? NO, SIR, I DID NOT.

Bedbugs are bad for a lot of reasons—the bites, the cost, having to explain to the dry cleaner that there might be eggs in your sweaters—but the worst thing about them is that they make you feel like you're doing something wrong. In a bedbug battle, nothing you do seems like it is ever enough. There's at least one bag full of clean clothes with a popped seal, one un-vacuumed crevice serving as a bedbug hideout, one errant book into whose pages a pregnant bug has escaped, prepared to launch a bedbug kingdom anew the minute you think you're safe. Internet forums are full of bedbug horror stories about people who live out of sterile bags for months, then finally return their clothing to their closets and drawers, only to find a plump little bastard hunkered down in a picture frame.

This sense that there's always more to do is difficult for perfectionists and people with OCD; it's also difficult for people who are ever cluttered and incomplete. I somehow simultaneously fall into all these camps, and so I am constantly punished. I want each crevice of my apartment dusted and poisoned and caulked into oblivion, but I can't be bothered to make the effort to do it until it's too late. I might go so far as to vacuum my room in an attempt to wrest eggs from my baseboards, but there's a good chance I'll fail to dispose of the bag with the utmost precaution. I remembered to put plastic around a throw pillow I tossed in the trash, but I forgot to seal it. I am a menace to my roommates, my neighbors, the entire borough of Brooklyn, and to myself.

When my Greenpoint apartment caught fire, people often asked me how I managed to handle that kind of devastating loss. Here's a fun fact: it was easier to deal with losing all my stuff in a fire than with bedbugs. When my apartment caught fire, it was like a death. It couldn't be helped or solved. There was nothing to treat. I had to accept that things were lost and briefly mourn them, then move on. Bedbugs are like an illness you have to test and treat and agonize over to fix. There is always a new medication to try, a new experimental treatment to undertake, a new tube to stick in your arm to see if it helps.

Then, of course, there's the fact that the fire was something that happened *to* me; I can't help but think that bedbugs are something I bring on myself. If you happen to be a friend of mine who is horrified to discover I'm secretly Brooklyn's Bedbug Mary, please note that (1) many exterminators have assured me that it is extremely unlikely I ever brought bedbugs to your house, so please do not send me any angry emails, and (2) I have probably been too ashamed to tell you about my several bedbug pets, because people who have bedbugs are dirty and messy and careless, and I feared even before I had bedbugs that you might think I am all of those things.

I am a perfectionist in that I will happily spend hours analyzing my two front teeth to measure exactly how much they've shifted in the last month (and will text photos of said teeth to my friends, family members, and you, dear stranger reading this essay, if you are unfortunate enough to provide me with your phone number). I will obsess over a mishung painting. I will count every gray hair. I will scrub at a single small clothing stain until I wear the fabric thin, making the mark even *more* obvious, because I am as much an idiot as a lunatic. Despite my best attempts, I'm imperfect all the time.

My friends own blow-dryers, clothing irons, and Tide to Go pens. They organize their books by color. They wipe down their laptop keyboards. They did not just purchase a brand-new tube of deodorant and promptly lose it in their bedroom. They don't forget to dump out the coffee filter for a week, then open it to discover it's cultivated a new ecosystem made of mold. They live in homes that are clean, either because they themselves are pristine or because they can afford to pay someone to do the dusting and vacuuming for them. They say things like, "Don't you think it's time to wash that tote bag, Rebecca?"

My friends can open a bag of chips without finishing the whole thing. My friends can eat half their sandwich and save the rest for tomorrow. My friends can cook. My friends can budget. My friends can go to a party and have one drink and go home. My friends would never drink too much and try to home-wreck a half-dead relationship. My friends can get others to tell them they love them and mean it. My friends are fully formed, fully functional human beings, and I am the Tasmanian devil, a frantic ball of insects and romantic disasters ready to whirl into your life and screw it up. My friends would never wake up at two A.M. and throw up on their bedroom floor.

I told all my friends when I had bedbugs the first time, and they looked at me sadly, because who else but me could contract this menace? People like me, who fling their clothes and problems and romantic pitfalls all over everything, don't just get bedbugs, they *deserve* them, and so my repetitive outbreaks are my fate, not just bad luck.

Of course, bedbugs don't discriminate—in theory, they infest the rich and put-together as much as they do the messy and penny-pinching. But that's hard to remember when you're once again living out of plastic bags and dropping books on pieces of lint that startle you in your living room. Indeed, here I am, sitting in my room in Brooklyn, wondering if the exterminators have managed to lay waste to the bloodsuckers in my box spring or if I'm doomed to live with these monsters until the end of time. I have been assured that they're mostly gone now and will be gone forever in two weeks, and that the only way to survive this is to give up control and "trust the process," which is hard to do when you can't even trust yourself to unplug the space heater before leaving the house.

Why Be Kind to Yourself When You Can Torture Your Mind Quietly?

Some experts say sports are a good way for children to build confidence. For me, sports—like forcing a comb through my hair for picture day or using scissors—were just another way to prove to myself how much shittier I was than all the other kids. I was scared of all the balls, even the soft foam ones they give toddlers to play with in day care. I ran too slow. I dribbled on my feet. I kicked to the wrong person. In an entire season of Jewish Community Center baseball, my bat made contact with the ball exactly once (it then hit one of the parents behind the foul line). I was the kid other kids groaned about when I ended up on their team. I was the player coaches tried to bench at crucial points in the game. Luckily, I liked the bench, where I could eat all the Oreos the soccer moms brought for halftime.

However, sport and exercise are not the same thing, and even though you'd have to threaten the members of my family I care about to get me to play soccer again, I do like to exercise. My father ran about a dozen marathons in his day, and when I was a wee tween he started taking me running with him, I assume because I was not good at Sport and therefore transforming into a dreaded sloth child. Though I loved sitting, it turned out I also loved running. I could run at my own pace, listen to my own music, and get lost in my own daydreams about finally Frenching eighth grade cutie Alex B. I wouldn't let down any teammates or subject myself to ridicule. I could just move and be without anyone bothering me or yelling at me to keep my eye on that hurling sphere of death called a ball.

Another thing I liked about running was that I could pretend I was good at it. I've never been a fast runner, but I was the only kid in my middle school doing it regularly, so while everyone else ran short sprints at basketball practice, I built up endurance. In high school, I started going on seven- or eight-mile runs in Central Park; in college, I ran endless loops around the fitness center's indoor track. Boys in school used to tell me they were "very impressed" by my dedication to the track, though they took back some of that praise as soon as they saw me try to lift a five-pound weight. In their adult years, a lot of my former non-running friends have started running half and full marathons while I rarely crack the five-mile mark, but I still like to run, and I don't care if they can all pass me now as long as I can do loops and daydream about Chris Pine uninterrupted.

One of the best things about running is that it's a pretty cheap form of exercise. All you need are a pair of running sneakers and a relatively carless, dogshit-less stretch of street or sidewalk. Runners don't need fancy equipment or a gym membership, except maybe in the winter, and even then you can usually get in a run as long as there's no ice on the ground and you set your alarm to EXTRA LOUD. When I was so addicted to running I'd get palpitations if I went a few days without it, I brought sneakers with me when I traveled and snuck in runs when I could. I learned a lot about running culture outside the United States, like that in Paris they don't have it, and in Italy they also don't have it and don't understand why you run when you could stand on the street and yell at someone for exercise instead.

So for a long time I prided myself on being my own gym, unbeholden to class schedules, hidden annual fees, and roaches that hide in the sauna. This self-sustaining smugness amplified when I moved back to

New York after college. As a woman living in North Brooklyn in the early 2010s, I discovered that yoga was inescapable. Bodegas transformed into yoga studios overnight. I got hit in the face with a rolled-up yoga mat every goddamn time I went to the grocery store. Half the conversations I'd overhear at bars were about "chaturanga-ing" and unfortunate physical ailments incurred during something called the camel pose.

Soon some of my best friends became yoga disciples, and they tried to get me into it, too. But I was, and still am, committed to the belief that yoga in the West is a scam, and I was not going to be taken in. My yogi pals spent upwards of $15 per class. I ran for free. They dropped mad bucks on henna yoga mats and swanky butterfly bras from Lululemon. I worked out in threadbare shorts I bought in middle school and a sports bra someone once mistook for my grandmother's.

Yoga and all its accoutrements were silly expenditures. And then, of course, there was the fact that I was bad at yoga. Once in college I ended up in an "advanced" class and could barely hold myself up in downward-facing dog, let alone manage a handstand. A few years later, a friend dragged me to an open level class in Bushwick, and I toppled on my face in half moon pose. Running was an exercise I could do without judgment, but yoga happened in a room full of strangers, all of whom would certainly see me tumble in a standing split and hear me fart in a squat. I'd spent my adult life avoiding my lack of athletic prowess, and I wasn't about to pay for a class that showcased it. So I stuck with running, while my friends went on to earn yoga instructor certifications and learn to enjoy kombucha.

When life is good and full of promise, a long run is the perfect thing. Runs give you time to let your mind wander unfettered. That kind of freedom lends itself well to, say, an exciting job prospect or an upcoming vacation or a flirty Gchat conversation with the co-worker you've been secretly lusting after for months. Flush with adrenaline, you're much more enthusiastic about logging several uphill miles in the heat. And all that time alone with your music and your brain is a breeding ground for your imagination, giving you space to map out whatever scenario of the future is currently spiking your heart rate.

My brain cares less about my career than it does about hot dudes, probably because I've occasionally experienced at least moderate success with the former. And so for me, running has always been at its best at the start of a crush, when the bad stuff hasn't happened yet and there's nothing but blue sky and daydreams. I reached the zenith of this phenomenon the spring I was twenty-four, when I developed a weird but niggling thing for a coworker.

Max was an adult—he was twenty-eight and had

lived with two former girlfriends, and he probably knew how to kiss without banging teeth. He also paid about 23 percent attention to me—i.e., smiled at me sometimes, let me smoke his weed, and Gchatted me links to pictures of cute dogs—which was just enough to suggest my fantasies about our making out in every corner of our Brooklyn office *could* come true, without forcing me to confront the horrible possibility that they *would.*

I decided I liked him about three years into our working relationship; one night we went to a bar for an ostensible quick post-work drink, and several hours later, somewhere deep in a pile of shoestring fries, it occurred to me that I didn't want to leave. I stayed out until close to midnight, pushing back very important plans to watch the *Veronica Mars* movie in favor of more face time with him.

For nearly ten months, my Max runs were a deep pleasure, rife with visions of desk sex, Chinese food, bad movie marathons, and blue-eyed babies. These daydreams were safe from the corruption of reality—I had no intention of revealing myself to Max, and so there was no opening for him to tell me he'd rather slice off a toe than engage in that desk sex with me. Real Max and I hardly spoke, giving Dream Max free run in my head.

And then, something startling happened: months

into penning diary entries that started with "Just like fuck literally everything, I don't even know," or "Another day, another chance to be ignored," or "Everything's stupid today. Everything sucks. I will never have sex again" (these tragically, are real), Max started to like me back. At first this was a good thing, and my runs went from far-flung fantasies to replays of recent events, like how he drove me home and checked out my ass at a party and flirted with me in the office and told a room full of strangers my favorite musical artist was Taylor Swift (it is not, but it is also not not, not that Guns N' Roses fans need to know this about me). One day we made out on a couch and in his car and in a bathroom stall at a bar in Park Slope, and my "Chinese food and babies forever" runs kicked it up to eleven. Were Dream Max and Reality Max on their way toward merging into one?

Not a fucking chance. Up front, Max made it clear I was nothing more than a fling. We worked together, he pointed out. We were friends. Why screw all that up by dating when we could hook up a few times instead? Current me might have been smart enough to sprint away from that cop-out, but then I was young and stupid and had wasted so much time on my fabricated Dream Max that I wasn't quite sure what to do with the living, breathing, thinking version who didn't want me enough.

You cannot make someone like you. You cannot

make someone stick around. This is something most people figure out quickly, but I slept with a security blanket until I was eighteen and am not good at separation. I feared that if Max and I did eventually sleep together, he'd flee me the instant he climaxed, and so I decided it would be best to pretend *I* was the one in control. I did this out of sheer terror. I was not ready to part with my imagined future.

It turns out trying to hang on to someone who doesn't want you will make you insane. One night a bunch of us went out in Brooklyn after work, and I drank six beers and made Max drive me home. It was then, with my brain mostly turned off, that I decided it would be a good idea to have a frank discussion about my feelings.

"You're not going to hurt me," I recall telling him as he wound down Bushwick's dark streets. "I'm going to hurt *you.* I'll destroy you."

"Um," Max said as he approached my building, "okay." He dropped me off and drove away.

Two days later, he met someone he liked, started dating her seriously, and neglected to tell me. He started throwing around the word *girlfriend* and invited her to his childhood home to meet his parents. I was informed of this burgeoning relationship several weeks into it, during drinks with yet another coworker, because when you shit where you eat, everyone around you slips in it. I cried in the cab home from the bar and then continued to cry nonstop for the next four months.

I had liked him so much I thought I would die if he didn't feel the same way. He didn't, and I didn't die, though I did spend weeks in daily hysterics on my couch, much to the chagrin of my poor roommate. But I could not escape him. At the office, I sat across from him for weeks on end. I listened to other people praise his work and his genius. I noted jokes he laughed at that were not mine. I overheard him drop hints about cute date nights with the woman he'd chosen over me. I remembered every minute of every single day that I was not enough, that someone else existed for him who filled my colossal gaps.

The long runs and free time to dream up the future transformed from pleasure to punishment, and I spent each mile envisioning the two of them unfurling further into each other's lives. Every step was a new form of pain. *He picked someone else. He is in love. He did not want me. He is happy without me,* I huffed uphill. On the way back, the self-torture: *Of course he doesn't want me. Who could want me? He's seen me eat. I am a monster.*

This wasn't the first bitter rejection. I get those like

headaches. But for months my secret pining had fueled my brain and body, and made me feel like there was something worth moving for, something more than the amorphous pile of anxieties—career? babies? home? the impending collapse of the Arctic glaciers that will eventually plummet us into a modern ice age???—that kept me up at night. Now the happy daydreams that consumed me were the cause of my pain, and I was left without any way to cope. I was in free fall. I could not escape the bad thoughts. I could not block out the image of them entangled supine in his bedroom on the lazy Sunday mornings I spent alone. I could not stop thinking about how all my daydreams belonged to someone else.

These cursed images didn't just pop up on runs, though certainly they dominated them. Indeed, they took up residence in my head at all times—when I woke up, when I brushed my teeth, when I showered, when I walked, when I rode the train, when I worked, when I breathed and swallowed and blinked my eyes. Every piece of me hurt—every muscle, every joint, every bone and tendon stiffened and ached and clenched in pain.

It occurred to me that I needed to stop thinking altogether. And so I went to a yoga class.

Westernized yoga is billed as an exercise class, but yoga is less about movement than stillness. Unlike running, yoga offers little to no room for your thoughts to wander. Serious yogis learn to sit and stand in poses for minutes and hours, focusing on their breath to stay sane. Yoga will make you strong and bendy, but it'll also teach you to quiet your mind, a welcome thing to master when your mind has become a weapon against you.

My yoga enthusiast friends had long been trying to sell me on this very theory: if I mastered crow pose, I'd get my brain to shut up for five seconds. I still wasn't thrilled by the prospect of tumbling over in public, but I was also desperate to stop the self-harm that had taken control of my headspace, so I accompanied one such enthusiast to a "gentle yoga" session.

"Gentle yoga" wasn't so gentle I didn't feel my bones break in my first warrior pose or pray for death in pigeon. It was also very hot (DID YOU KNOW THEY HEAT YOGA CLASSES???!!), and at the end of the session my mat looked like a crosswalk in a rainstorm. But no one sneered at me when I struggled to hold myself up or bent my knee in the wrong way, and I felt surprisingly stretched out when the hour was done. I decided to start going to a beginner's class, then graduated to a regular class, then eventually signed up for a monthly membership at a yoga studio near my apartment, which smelled like incense and was full of lithe instructors who recognized my face.

It turns out no one cares if you suck at yoga. All that matters in class is what's going on with you on your mat, since everyone's deep in their own shit, and no one has time to think about what a crappy job someone else is doing when they're fighting back tight-hamstring tears. Some people can twist themselves into boneless little knots, and some people can't touch their toes. No one gives a fuck who does what. If you want to bend your body into a full wheel, be my guest. If you believe *strongly*, despite the absence of any evidence, that doing so will curse you with premature arthritis, you can put your legs up the wall instead. No matter how hard you work or how much time you spend luxuriating in child's pose, at the end we all lie on the ground in the final resting pose—that is to say, Adult Naptime.

Sometimes in class you chant together for a few minutes, which can be nice or it can be stupid and performative, depending on the mood you're in. Sometimes the instructor reads an "uplifting" mantra or prompt, which can be nice or pretentious. Sometimes at the end of class, when you're done with Adult Naptime but aren't quite ready to face the world of the Awake, the instructor tells you to roll onto your right side in the fetal position and feel the ground support you underneath, which can be soothing and restorative or piss you off because you've needed to pee since the second sun salutation and you know you'll have to sit through at least three collective *om*s before you can utter *Namaste* and hit the bathroom stall.

When I first started doing yoga, though, I leaned in hard to the chanting and positive reinforcement. I looked forward to lying in a fetal position on the floor. When the only thoughts you yourself can create comprise a continuous stream of self-flagellation, it's useful to have a stranger tell you you're strong and powerful, even if they're just doing it because it's their job. "Speak kindly to yourself," the teachers would intone as we sat cross-legged in a candlelit room. "You are powerful. You are strong. You are supported. You are enough."

None of these yoga instructors knew me, and certainly if they'd seen me try to unscrew a jar, they'd have reconsidered some of their meditations. But at this point I was spending approximately a fifth of my waking hours sobbing on my couch and wishing I were dead, and so the few hours a week I got to stretch in a quiet room and have someone call me powerful were a real respite, even if I had to return to the darkness once I rolled up my mat.

I didn't get much better at handstands in my first few months as a weekly-to-twice-weekly yoga practitioner, but I did get better at focusing on the breath, at least if I internally screamed at myself to focus each time I found my mind wandering. Meditation really did have its benefits. Outside of yoga, if I found my brain starting to unspool into a spiral of self-hate, I'd make myself breathe, just as I did in a particularly challenging (that is to say, any) pose. When late at night, passing thoughts like "I should uninstall my air conditioner" escalated into "Oh my god, I'm twenty-five and single and going to die alone while bedbugs feast on my eyeballs," I'd curl into a fetal position and whisper to myself that I was enough. It was hokey and it wasn't necessarily true, but it calmed me nonetheless.

Max and I continued to work together, which was sometimes fine and other times so unpleasant I considered quitting on the spot. He faded in and out as I embarked on other, equally unwise flings. We kept up the Gchats and dog photos. I met his girlfriend, who was perfectly nice. I lent him my favorite book, and he refused to give it back. When we stopped working together, he stopped talking to me. Eventually I stopped thinking about him, though every so often I missed what it felt like to be so consumed.

It would be cool to say that yoga taught my brain to shut up and transformed my body into a temple of tranquility and killer abs, but less than a year after I started practicing regularly, I regressed into my old lazy, undisciplined self. I abandoned my monthly membership after the fire forced me to move, and though I found new studios scattered throughout the city, once I had to pay for classes à la carte, I stopped bothering to go twice a week. Yoga is still stupid expensive.

Now if I make it to two yoga classes a month, I feel like a superhero. And my dumb, loud brain, once so duly trained, has gone back to being dumb and loud, so when I do go to class, I can't seem to focus on the breath. Instead, I focus on everything: dinner, my credit card bill, puppies, whether or not eggs are baby chickens, the old lady I saw eating alone at the ramen place, how depressing it is that Johnny Depp is such a creep now, that really fucking good show *Fleabag*, orgasms. This makes the time pass, but it doesn't make me good at yoga, and I still can't do a goddamn handstand.

What I am good at, though, is sitting in the pain. They say your yoga pose doesn't begin until you want to get out of it, and if you've got tight muscles and find yourself stuck in a split or a lizard pose, you want to get out of it FAST. When you sit with your screaming hamstrings long enough, the pain grows until you want to die—and then, just when you think you can't take another fucking second, the pain starts to lessen. I assume it's because your muscle is now stretched or because you've successfully shattered a nerve, but either way, it works. There's a lot to be learned from sitting with the pain—on the mat with your leg bent weird, or at a bar with a former colleague, learning your old flame got engaged to that girlfriend over the summer. A year ago that would have made you scream with agony, but now the pain passes through you so you can go back to thinking about the snacks you're going to pick up on the way home.

Everything in Moderation, Especially Moderation

One of Charlie Chaplin's greatest films is *City Lights,* a 1931 silent picture about a Tramp who falls in love with a blind woman. The Tramp goes to great and often comedic lengths to trick the blind woman into thinking he's wealthy. At one point in the film, he saves a drunken millionaire from dying by suicide. The millionaire invites the Tramp in, declares he's his best friend, lends him money and a car, and fetes him all night. In the morning, though, the millionaire is sober and has no memory of the Tramp. He throws him out. Later, drunk, the millionaire invites the Tramp back in. In the morning, the cycle is repeated.

I watched *City Lights* with my grandparents as a very young child, and though I don't remember much else about the plot, I remember the drunken million-aire. "Why doesn't he know the Tramp?" I asked my grandfather after the millionaire first tossed Chaplin out. "Because alcohol makes you forget what hap-pened," my grandfather said. "So does he not want to be friends with the Tramp?" I asked. "I don't know," my grandfather said. "You don't know whether he's his real self when he's sober or drunk." The millionaire's life seemed exciting. I stuck him permanently some-where in my brain.

I was fifteen the first time I really tried alcohol. As a kid I'd been allowed one or two sips of wine or beer, but my parents aren't really drinkers, so I never had a drink of my own as a youth. But I was curious as a teen, about alcohol and about the promise of rebellion, and one night, just a few weeks into my sophomore year of high school, my friend and I had a shot or two of her mother's Grand Marnier on a sleepover. I liked the way the alcohol warmed me up and blurred all the edges. We stayed up late watching dumb movies and feeling our fingers tingle until the magic wore off, and when I went home the next morning I felt grown-up and alive.

Even before that first illicit sip of Grand Marnier, I understood that alcohol made things happen. Alcohol helped people reveal themselves, and it made them do things they otherwise feared. One of my favorite movies as a kid was *10 Things I Hate About You,* a classic retelling of Shakespeare's *Taming of the Shrew,* but with Padua reimagined as a grunge-era Seattle high school. In one scene, Heath Ledger chases heroine Julia Stiles to a party; she ends up taking tequila shots to combat whatever fucked-up teen angst the film's writers had bubbling inside her, and falls off a table while dancing to Biggie. The nineties! Ledger takes her out of the house and puts her on a swing, and she tells him he has pretty eyes before throwing up on his feet. Tween me watched that scene over and over again. I thought it was beautiful.

There were so many of these moments in my pop culture–smeared youth. In *The Wedding Planner,* Matthew McConaughey falls for Jennifer Lopez when she gets drunk and cries to him about running into her ex and his pregnant wife. In *Working Girl,* Harrison Ford's and Melanie Griffith's meet-cute happens because she gets bombed at a networking event. Ross and Rachel get married drunk in Vegas. Songs I loved were about drinking whiskey and feeling blue. When Sam cracks a beer after losing his lucky bottle cap on *Cheers,* I was disappointed he didn't take a drink. I wanted to see him at his most vulnerable.

I entered high school believing that alcohol would help me be who I wanted to be, not who I was. When I started drinking, alcohol did become a friend. At parties, where boys made out with my pretty classmates but not me, alcohol smoothed out the baby fat bulging from under my tank tops and convinced me that gobs of MAC lip gloss made me beautiful.

Alcohol was an equalizer. When I was sober, it was a chore to find stuff to talk about with the people at school I didn't know if I liked, but a cup of vodka with a splash of Diet Coke loosened my tongue and made our slurred conversations about how drunk we all were seem seamless. Even kids I didn't know talked to me when they were drunk and I was, too, the effects of distilled ethanol bonding us together in a shared stupid euphoria. When we were drinking, we all loved *this song*. We all loved *your shirt*. We all loved *each other* and we *always would*. Until the morning, of course, when we hated everyone and also sunlight.

Alcohol, like my high school friends themselves, was also an enemy. It made everything blurry but also intense. One time I watched a boy I liked make out with another girl at a dance and burst into sad drunk tears while wailing, "MY LIFE IS OVER!" in front of him and everyone else. Another time I got so drunk at a party I threw up on my friend's parents' Persian carpet, then spent the rest of the night throwing up in a bucket while someone's mother (not mine) held back my hair. And then there was my talent for the art of blacking out—when I drank too much, I started to notice missing patches of memory, which served as a warning that a part of me I didn't know had time to wreak havoc upon the world unfettered. I couldn't remember riding in elevators or getting in cabs or crying in public or, to be frank, regurgitating all that vodka on the aforementioned carpet. But someone did all those things. I was told it was me.

•

In college, I stopped blacking out, probably because I regularly drank *so* much that my bloodstream became accustomed to comprising 80 percent Everclear. Freshman year, we put vodka in Tropicana juice bottles and drank in our dorm rooms until we couldn't see straight, still somehow managing to make it to Cognitive Psychology in the morning (I got a C+, *thank you very much*). We drank jungle juice out of plastic cups in beer-soaked basements and stained our going-out shirts from Urban Outfitters with amaretto sours spilled at bars that let us in with our underage college IDs. We were drunk all the time—in class, in the library, on the quad, and at least once, in the emergency room at the hospital down the street.

College cemented my tween thesis that alcohol makes things happen. My first night on campus, I drank four beers and kissed a boy at a fraternity party—a rare occurrence in high school, but apparently easy in a place where alcohol made me brave around strange men. Not long into my first semester, I developed a crush on someone in my friend group and convinced him to hook up with me one booze-soaked October night.

He told me he wasn't into me, but after nights out drinking together, we tended to end up fooling around. Sometimes I pretended I was drunker than I was so he'd have to take care of me, like all good romcom protagonists. Was this plan stupid? Absolutely, but it also worked. Alcohol made me not me, or maybe it made me a better me, it was hard to know. Either way, it made me a me he occasionally wanted to see naked. Intoxication was the key to our "romance," a fact made all the more evident one night when we made out in his room sans booze.

"I know we hooked up sober, but I don't want to confuse you," he texted me later that night. *I guess I won't be sober next time*, I thought. And I wasn't. In the end, he still dumped me, probably to date someone he didn't have to watch puke in a dorm room trash can. I spent the rest of college drinking with men I liked a lot less.

•

Somewhere in adulthood, I went from being a bad drunk to a worse one. The rampant tears, vomiting, and memory loss that plagued me as a drunk teen seem to return from time to time now that I have allegedly grown up. It is possible this is because I drink less now. It is possible it's because I drink more. Whatever the case, this is not my best quality. It is way less cute to act like an intoxicated idiot when you're nearing thirty, not that it was adorable when I was fifteen. On a good day, the worst thing I'll do in public when I drink too much is announce that I want to have sex with Ted Cruz. On a very bad one, my brain will go dark right before I tell a present male body I love him, and I'll regain consciousness in the midst of throwing up out a cab window.

New York is not a place to learn to cut back. Here you can drink every single day, mostly at all hours, and though bartenders claim they'll kick you out if you pass out with your head on a table, experience has taught me that's not the case. I worked evenings my first year out of school and didn't drink much, but when I was twenty-three and lived in Bushwick, my apartment was directly across the street from a very popular bar, which was the death of me. I used to go out drinking elsewhere, come home tanked, meet more friends for more beers across the street, stay out until four, make out with a mistake, and somehow make blogs in the morning, because youth is a gift.

Things started going downhill for real when I began working regularly for the internet. I am four-eleven and 108 pounds, and as you've probably surmised, alcohol in vast quantities turns me into a destructive force. But if I manage to get the measurements just right—the amount of booze, the quantity of food, some semblance of emotional stability—alcohol makes my life a little easier. I am a socially anxious person, so much so that even calling a doctor's office to make an appointment makes my ribs sweat. It turns out drinking is a great way to combat that kind of social anxiety.

A few glasses of wine or sixteen beers lubricates the part of my brain that otherwise screams when a stranger asks me a question, and also convinces me that I am a fascinating person to talk to, even if everything I say is slurred and I can't remember it later anyway. And so when I started drinking with the staff writers at the blog that wouldn't give me a full-time job—all of whom were older than me and seemed like real grown-ups, not fake ones who managed to burn pasta and did not own window shades—I tried to keep up with them, to prove I deserved a place among them, the Real People.

As was the case with my high school compatriots, the more I drank with these writers, the more cohesive we felt, as if we were real friends and colleagues, like I wasn't just playacting Adult, but had finally become one. We all hated *our jobs*, we all hated *New York*, but we all loved *us*, and we always would, until morning, when we had to fight hangovers and one another over the good story pitches.

The drinking didn't stop when I was finally hired full time. If anything, it got worse, now that I'd earned my spot. We took shots at five P.M. We kept Fireball in our desks. Happy hours were abundant. I mixed whiskey with tequila, weed candy, and PBR. The blackouts started rolling back in, like the time I drank a cup of Scotch in our Brooklyn office after work and came to eating dumplings somewhere in Chinatown. Another time, I spilled my beer on a stranger in a bar and threatened to fight him. Or so I was told later, as I sobered up in the cab home.

•

A six-four dude with at least a hundred pounds on me recently asked me what it's like to black out, since his body mass and possibly less destructive relationship with booze seems to prevent him from having this kind of intermittent nightmare. "Do you remember anything?" he said. "Do you see snippets, or is the night just gone?" I imagine it's different for everyone, but for me, it's a little bit of both. Memories of a blackout are like scenes from a student film, with no words and bad cuts, the tape crinkled and looped in weird places. I end up in the middle of a conversation I don't recall starting, in rooms I can't remember walking into, on the street on my way home when I am certain I was just on someone's roof. Chunks of the night flit in and out of my brain like a dream, but I'm awake and in public and everyone else just saw me drop a full glass on the ground.

The pieces that are missing, though, are gone. According to scientists, blackouts likely occur when alcohol suppresses the hippocampus, making it very difficult or impossible for the brain to create a coherent record of events. The brain no longer makes memories, and so while you might be functioning and talking and breathing and walking and making out with a stranger as if all is well, when you play the tape back later, sections show nothing but dead air.

Each time I've blacked out, I begged my friends not to tell me what I did or said. Maybe it would be better if they did—maybe it would scare me into permanent sobriety or at least convince me to binge-eat pasta before my own birthday parties—but blacking out is a bit like being under hypnosis. Someone once took a video of me explaining the intricacies of the G train after I had five martinis at a vodka-related press event, and when he showed it to me later, I needed a full three days to recover. Sure, it was my voice making sounds and my face making shapes, but the part of me that lives inside and makes choices about the sounds and shapes that come out didn't seem to be there at all.

•

Lest you think that all I do with my drinking life is pass out at the First Avenue L train stop, note that that has happened ONLY ONE TIME. In my many years of drinking, I have learned to do certain things to spare myself humiliation and two-day hangovers. I eat dinner now. I alternate booze and seltzer. I drink Pedialyte at weddings. I drink less. For the most part, I am a charming drunk, more sociable than when I'm sober, more unrestrained than when the brain cells that make fear are firing at full capacity.

What I love about alcohol is that it takes me out of my own head, a place in which I do not recommend people spend a lot of time. In addition to the hippocampus, alcohol impairs the frontal lobe, which is basically the brain's control panel and is in charge of making choices about everything from whether you should take your clothes off and go skinny-dipping in the Lincoln Memorial Reflecting Pool, to whether you should have sex on the literal street with a tourist you met at a pub crawl in Prague. Not saying I've done either! But if I have, it's because booze made the part of my brain that's afraid of everything afraid of nothing. (That part of the brain, says science, is the amygdala, and yep, booze impairs it, too. And yes, I *should* have gotten at least a B in cognitive psych.)

While the two aforementioned examples (that may or may not have really happened!) might be extreme, it is true that drinking has gifted me with some adventures, perhaps because when I drink I'm not me, or maybe I'm the real me. It's hard to know which one of me is who I am.

If the drunk me is the real me, though, she is also terribly unhappy. I blacked out on my twenty-eighth birthday and cried. I blacked out at a work holiday party once and cried. I blacked out at a fake work holiday party and cried. I blacked out in my own apartment while eating a burrito in the bathroom, then threw up on the floor and cried. Even when I stay conscious, the alcohol's depressive properties have me sobbing on trains and street corners and wondering in my darker moments if it's worth it to keep going on.

•

I thought losing my job would take me from serious problem drinker to full-blown alcoholic, but somehow it spurred me to cut back. Not in the immediate aftermath of my layoff—I'm not actually sure the last two months of 2017 even happened—but by midwinter I started going days and weeks without booze. It turns out drinking makes me pretty stupid, and I enjoyed the extra brain space that came with temperance. Words started coming to me faster, I had more energy, and I shed at least a small bit of the depression that had followed me around for a decade. I was also extremely well hydrated, thanks to all the soda waters I drank at bars so I'd have something to hold while everyone around me pounded Miller High Lifes, the champagne of unemployed journalists. My skin looked *great*.

You'd think all that clearheadedness would inspire me to stop drinking forever, but quasi-sobriety was boring. I am not me if I'm not an occasional intoxicated mess. Last month I got drunk and slept with someone who has a girlfriend. Last week I skipped dinner, blacked out on a friend's rooftop, and hit on at least several attendees (I probably also cried).

I know I'm an addict. I'm not literally addicted to booze. I am a hard and functional worker. I am not stashing airplane bottles of Jack Daniel's in my bedroom. I can go weeks without drinking and not feel any withdrawal effects save for clarity. But I'm addicted to how I feel when I drink—like I'm not me or I'm a better me, or at least I'm more alive than the sober me who's too afraid to ask the world for what she wants. When I'm drunk, I take it, even if I take it too far.

Am I embarrassed? Certainly. Do I hate myself?

Usually. Do I wish I were someone who could be exciting on her own, without a shot or six of liquid courage to aid her in inevitable self-destruction? All the time. But this is who I am. Or at least it's who I think I am. I'm not sure, at this point, that there's a difference.

Misery Loves
No Company at All

My two favorite sex positions are missionary and sleeping alone.*

One might argue that sleeping alone is not in fact a sex position, but it gives me almost as much pleasure as sex itself. Sometimes it gives me more, because sexual experiences, like men in general, tend to be disappointing. It is a luxury to sleep alone. I shared a room with my sister for our entire childhood, in part

---

*I know everyone's crazy about backward cow horse or Wax Alien or whatever, but missionary is underrated. It's not fancy, but it feels like I'm getting a big hug, and I don't have to do any of the work. It was also my first sex position (and for way too long, my only one), so I know how to do it, or at the very least I haven't gotten any specific complaints. If you have any, please direct them to my publisher.

because we lived in a small apartment, and in part because my mother claimed it would "make it easier" for us when we grew up and had to share space with a romantic partner. My mother is not in any way a professional child psychologist, and this tactic backfired big-time. The day I got my own room, I swore I would never share another, and I have mostly held true to this, much to my ovaries' chagrin.

It is great to sleep alone. When you sleep alone, no one makes noise but you. You can sniffle and snore and rustle and pass gas all you want. When you sleep by yourself, nobody breathes in your ear or shakes you awake or cares if it takes three hours of *Buffy the Vampire Slayer* YouTube fan videos to put you to bed. Every time I spend the night with someone or someone spends the night with me, I end up hoping my bed buddy will stop breathing in his sleep, and I can only assume it's the same for them. This extends beyond romantic partners. A few weeks ago, a friend and I shared a bed at a wedding in Boston. Neither of us slept much, we each snored when we did, and in the morning everyone was cranky.

I'm not the only person who knows the joys of solo sleep. According to the U.S. census, unmarried men and women make up 47.6 percent of total households in the United States, totaling about 110.6 million Americans. Sixty-three percent of those single Americans have never been married. And for women seeking men, the odds aren't good—there are 88 single men for every 100 single women. Back in Charles Dickens's time, spinsters were invisible undesirables whose fathers got stuck supporting them because they were too plain or picky or unusual, or because one treacherous lover rendered them clad in their doomed wedding dress for life. Now women can support themselves; skyrocketing divorce rates have shattered the myth of One True Love, of Happily Ever After, of Happy as a goal you hit at the altar and attain forever.

So we seek solace in friendships—long-term friends, friends born out of convenience, friends we bonded with last week on the bathroom line and will probably forget about in three days. And we seek solace in ourselves, because no matter how many group dinners you plan and brunches you eat and parties you attend, it is still possible that everyone around you will disappear.

•

The truth is, I am often alone now, not just when I sleep. Once upon a time, though, I was almost never alone. I had coworkers and happy hour buddies and weekend friends with whom I spent way too much money at the Meatball Shop. I had roommates who spent whole days and evenings marathoning bad movies and episodes of *Friday Night Lights* with me. I had men who "stopped by" on Saturday nights to steal my attention, then later summarily dumped me. I had confidantes who met me at bars to share stories about the men who stole our attention and later summarily dumped us. I was very busy.

Even when I had all these friends and coworkers clamoring to clog up my calendar, I feared that I would lose them. I worried all the time that my girlfriends would find boyfriends, that my man friends would find girlfriends, that the men I liked would find other women to fill their heads—that each and every one of my acquaintances would abandon me for better options. In my solitary future, I would become that sad woman who ate alone at restaurants while the happy people pointed at her and laughed. I would die in my apartment, carpet beetles nibbling at my decaying flesh, while everyone else was at brunch.

As luck would have it, that paralyzing fear of abandonment did in fact come to fruition. When I was young—you know, like two years ago—people told me the good times would come to an end. "You lose friends as you get older," they said. "Also, no one will date you after you turn thirty." I still have one more fuckable year to waste, but I have already noticed a precipitous drop in friends. Some of my old go-tos did find serious partners and, in folding these partners into their lives, tumbled out of mine. Some moved to Los Angeles. Some just moved uptown, but they might as well have moved to Los Angeles.

Some disappeared on their own, because once we didn't work together or live together or commute on the same train line, we didn't have all that much tying us to one another. When we met up on occasion, we'd reminisce about our old connections, but beyond that and a superficial catch-up, hangouts were too pitted with awkward silences to warrant second attempts. It is strange when a friend becomes a stranger. You've grown too distant to share with each other the warts and vulnerabilities that make a person real, but you remember what it was like when you saw them unpeeled.

Sometimes these friends disappear without your noticing, until one day they reappear and you realize how far you've drifted from each other. A few years ago, I went to a party hosted by a former college classmate. We'd been close at school, sharing our crushes and heartbreaks and unending insecurities; but once we left the nest, the real world was for us to compete. When we'd meet up, it was just an opportunity to measure our successes, or maybe it was just me with something to prove. We stopped being real friends, and soon ceased seeing each other in general.

I can't remember why exactly I decided to go to this particular party. I was in the middle of one of my many romantic crises, and when that happens, I say yes to invites as a rule in case I manage to meet someone I can use to make the object of my affection jealous. Perhaps that was my reasoning. Whatever the deal, I went.

She was surprised to see me. "Oh, hello!" she said, eyes wide, when she opened the door. "You came!" I smiled and started to tell her I missed her, when she squealed and brushed past me to hug someone she liked better.

I recognized some people at the party—other folks I went to school with but no longer really knew, and friends of this friend I'd spent time with when our lives were intertwined. And there were a lot of people I didn't know. They had inside jokes, secrets, stories, and questions for my former friend that I did not share and could not understand. I spent most of the night alone by the cheese. It was weird to witness firsthand that I did not know her anymore. When your life moves on from a job or a place or a kind of person you were, someone else keeps living and changing and experiencing without you. It's not bad or good, but it is.

There are lots of friends like that—the ones you lose slowly because it no longer makes sense to stay friends. And there are the friends who throw you out, which happens fast. One of my best friends from college dumped me over email a few years ago. We had a fight over something stupid—veganism, maybe, or the color she should dye her hair—but the important thing was that my insecurities and self-flagellation were toxic to her, and she did not want to put up with it anymore.

I dismissed it at first. *She's the crazy one,* I thought, writing her an email outlining all the reasons she was wrong. But she was right. At that moment in time I was selfish, self-obsessed (shocking, truly), and toxic to her, and in her efforts to mitigate the toxicity, she became toxic to me. I don't miss her, not because she was a bad friend (though I think I might have been) but because when someone exits your life like that, you have to let them go.

•

This is not to say I have no friends. For some reason, people still want to talk to me, though perhaps they will feel less inclined now that they know how many times I've had bedbugs. But friendships are different when you are no longer afraid of being alone. When I was twenty-two, I clung to the people around me, because without them there was only me, and I wasn't much company. There was safety in numbers. It wasn't just you who got dumped or freaked out over money or feared all the time that life wouldn't turn out the way you wanted it to, but *all* of you, who navigated the madness hand in hand. To spend an evening alone meant I *was* alone, and I'd have way too much time to think about how I always might be.

Of course, in many respects, I am never alone. People are goddamn everywhere. I live with two roommates in a tiny apartment, and though I fantasize each day about residing somewhere where I don't have to listen to another person have sex, unless I sell all my earthly possessions or move to deep Staten Island, I will never be able to afford my own place. I reside in a city with over eight million people, and every single day I bump into at least three of them on the sidewalk because I refuse to look up from my phone while walking, lest I miss one of Cher's tweets. Every day I am crushed between human bodies on the subway or kept awake by bodies breaking up outside my bedroom window or infected with the flu by a body sneezing near me at the coffee shop. I am never free of the reminder that there are billions of people out there, which only serves to heighten my awareness of my relative aloneness.

The funny thing about my erstwhile fear of being alone was that I never really feared being lonely. I just didn't want everyone else to have fun without me. I didn't want my friends to get boyfriends and husbands and babies and leave me behind. I didn't want to miss out on what it would mean to share a life with someone else, to fall in love and make a family and grow old surrounded by loved ones like you were supposed to do.

I'm not sure that path is where I'm headed, or if it's

even where I want to go. I'm not sure it's what I wanted back when I feared I wouldn't get it, or if I just didn't want to feel left out. But that fear got lost somewhere, along with the old friends whose lives no longer fit mine. Life happens all the time, even if you don't get to post 10,000 Instagram photos each week reminding everyone you just got engaged.

•

I have mentioned my captivation with the concept of *cogito, ergo sum*—I think, therefore I am—in terms of how it played out with anxiety, but it also has practical applications. When my mind broke at nineteen, I liked its suggestion that nothing existed beyond the borders of your own brain because it let me avoid scary things like death, war, and my macroeconomics exam, because none of those things were real if the *cogito* held true. I also liked it because it let me be a bad and selfish person. I could stand up dates and talk shit about nice people and not recycle, because nothing mattered except me.

I still like the *cogito*, but not for the same reasons. I don't think it means that no one outside my head exists or even matters, so much as it's a reminder that the person you matter most to is yourself. That is not an excuse to stick straws up sea animals' noses, but it is an excuse to stop fearing you'll be the last one left without a partner in crime. No matter how many people flit in and out of your life, you'll always be stuck with yourself.

It is always possible that I will meet someone, fall in love, make a baby, and raise it in a Park Slope brownstone purchased with our shared incomes. Anything can happen at any moment, as I am frequently reminded every time I have to tell my landlord the ceiling fell in. But it is also possible I won't.

Maybe learning not to fear solitude will make it easier for me to give it up somewhere down the road. Maybe, when I'm older and wiser and past my prime, I'll decide to let someone in because I want them, not because I'm afraid of missing out on something or being left behind. Maybe I won't. Maybe all my friends will find love or move to Los Angeles or move uptown and forget about me. Maybe I will spend every day alone until the carpet beetles attack. It could be worse. I could have to listen to someone else snore.

How to Fail at Failing

I should probably start this off by admitting that I am spoiled as shit. Though I now panic over money at least twice an hour, I grew up in a nice apartment on the Upper West Side of Manhattan, and I spent my teen years complaining about having to save my babysitting dollars to buy one stupid overpriced jean jacket at J.Crew. At the time, I considered this to be a struggle. Which was, of course, deeply incorrect. But I was (and often still am) blind to real struggle, though never as blind as the year I matriculated at a fancy New York City private high school that was full of Very Rich People.

The Very Rich People took me by surprise. Before the Upper West Side, I lived in pre-Giuliani Midtown Manhattan, where public schools were allegedly "not good," so it was decided I would attend private school. Real private school was very expensive, so instead, from nursery through eighth grade, I went to a then-unfancy Jewish day school. There were a few Very Rich People hiding out among my classmates, but the majority were the children of social workers, teachers, rabbis, and other folks in comfortable, but not lucrative, careers. It was a nice place to grow up, despite the fact that they taught us about the Holocaust alongside the primary colors.

New York City has some of the best private high schools in the country. Classes are intimate, teachers are dynamic, and the college guidance counselors have "special" relationships with admissions officers at the most coveted universities. By the time I was in eighth grade, I yearned for an experience beyond my forty-person-per-grade Jewish school, plus I was tired of pretending I'd never eaten shrimp. I applied to a bunch of those fancy schools, and when it came time to start ninth grade, I headed to a prestigious prep school in Riverdale, complete with ball fields (!!!), a swimming pool (!!!!!!!!!), multiple buildings for learning (!!!!!!!!!!!!!!!!!!!), and a surprising number of students with personal drivers.

Annual tuition for these schools is now up to about $40,000 per year, and though my school cost much less than that when I entered in 2003, it was, I believe, still too expensive for my parents. My grandparents had the money, and so they paid for me (and later, for my sister) to attend this school. I both didn't quite know this at the time and also did. But cost-prohibitive or not, it was important for me to go there if I wanted to go places. And if I didn't go places, it wouldn't just be me I'd be letting down. There was, after all, an entire tribe standing behind me, pushing me forward.

•

New York City private school is not quite as crazy as it looks on *Gossip Girl*—there are fewer murder plot lines and I don't recall ever attending a catered brunch or someone's wedding to a prince. But there were big drunken parties. Skinny attendees of all-girls schools whom all the hot boys wanted to fuck hung around those parties. Kids probably did coke in the school bathrooms, not that anyone invited me. People knew what Fabergé eggs were, because their parents owned them. I'm sure at least one person lived in a hotel.

I was startled by the drivers and the four-floor penthouses and the bathroom coke I heard about but never saw. All of this was new to me. The other thing that was new was the academic pressure. I was here to excel—that was the point, after all, of pouring money into private school tuition. In theory, I had worked hard to get into this school; my parents had worked hard to help me work hard to get into it, and my grandparents had worked hard to pay for it.

Hard work here would get me to into a good college; hard work there would get me into a good graduate school, and hard work in grad school would get me a job to pay for the next generation's private education. This was how it worked. This is what was necessary to succeed. Armed with this knowledge, I started my new school.

•

At my teeny day school it was easy for me to be somewhere near the top of my class, but at this behemoth, excelling was a challenge. I am not as smart as I think I am, and I don't like to work hard at things that don't come easy. At my old school, there was an entire science unit that focused on determining which methods of cow slaughter were kosher. Here we had biology. The textbooks had real science words, like *cytokinesis* and *petri dish*. It took some adjusting.

In ninth grade I did all the reading and raised my hand in class and generally enjoyed getting As and nice comments on all my essays, just as I did at my old school. But in tenth grade, I somehow ended up in three advanced courses, two of which were Algebra II and Chemistry. Numbers have long been my nemeses. On the SATs, I added 8 and 6 and got 4. But my academic adviser (fancy school!) told me college admissions officers preferred students who got lower grades in a hard class than high ones in a mediocre one, even if the former triggered regular night sweats. I had my little heart set on Brown, the only university in the United States of America, so I decided to stick out the scary numbers.

On my first advanced chemistry test, I got a C. On the second one, I got a C−. On the third, I did so poorly I had to retake the test, and I did so poorly on the retake that I had to have a meeting with the teacher, who tried very patiently to explain covalent bonds (fancy school!). In Algebra II, my worksheets and exams came back with bold *68*s circled at the top. I continued to try to understand the numbers and symbols, but they swam together and twisted and jumbled in front of me on the page. Even when I studied for more hours than I currently spend bingeing on all eleven seasons of *Cheers*, my tests came back tattooed in red ink.

"I think this class is too hard for you," one of my teachers told me gently. "You're failing." It was strange to hear. I had never failed anything before.

•

What they don't tell you when you're young and afraid of failing is that it is very freeing to fail. It is even more freeing when you fail in full than when you fail in part. It's easier to scrap something entirely than to fix something that's broken, which is why couples break up after their first fight and no one ever eats half a burger. If you can't be the best, you might as well be the worst. The resignation is liberating.

When I started to fail math and chemistry, I stopped paying attention in class and doing my homework. I didn't study for tests. The damage had been done, and it didn't matter anymore. I was no longer the smartest, so I was no longer smart. No amount of hard work or focus or hours spent reading my textbook was going to make me understand quadratic equations. Now I had more time to watch TV.

It was so nice not working hard at math and science that I did the same for my other classes, which were much easier for me but still required me to put in some effort. There are no walls to cling to in a free fall. I stopped doing the reading for my English lit class. I stopped studying for history tests. I lost my Spanish book. I faked sick during first period and hung out in the nurse's office. I faked sick in the morning before the bus came and stayed home on my couch. Teachers in even my strong subjects started picking up on my lack of preparation, perhaps because I called *Walden* a "very good book." My grades tanked, and I went from a mostly effortless A student to someone who had to have parents sign her tests. Such is the maturity of a fifteen-year-old tasked with making good on a very adult financial investment: I fucking loved it.

•

Also pertinent: the summer before tenth grade, I discovered the Doors. One day my father played "Light My Fire" on the stereo, and all was lost. I thought Jim Morrison was the hottest cat on the block, assuming the block had transported back through time, since he'd been dead for over three decades when I heard of him.

I listened to a song he recorded while tripping on acid, and one he recorded while getting a blow job. He sang about eating out women and anal sex and getting "higher," all of which were things I didn't quite understand but knew I would soon. I read about how he spent the summer of 1965 living on a friend's rooftop in Venice Beach and stealing oranges from neighbors' trees. He was bohemian and free, a blend of SEX and DRUGS and LOVE and LIVING, even though he was not actually living, and so to me he offered the promise of the wild life just out of reach.

That fall I got drunk for the first time. Two weeks later, I tried pot in the backyard of one of my classmates' fancy apartments, the kind with columns at the entrance and multiple floors outfitted with built-in bookshelves. Somewhere in this period, I also developed a crush on a classmate named Jake. He also loved Jim Morrison. He'd had sex already and smoked a lot of weed, and did terribly in school, and sometimes during our free periods we'd share clove cigarettes in a park near campus. He had no interest in me, or maybe he was just interested enough in having a girl like him that he kept me on the hook, I'm not sure.

But I know I started living and breathing him, so much so that I posted entries composed entirely of Doors lyrics on my (very public) online journal to exemplify my love. "'Can you picture what we'll be,'" I typed to the music. "'So limitless and free. . . . This is the end.'" This was, again, all public. I know you would have hated me in high school. Don't worry, I hated me, too.

When I started failing, I felt like a rebel, the way Jake was, the way Jim Morrison must have been, considering the number of times he got arrested for indecent exposure. I felt like Not Me, like a braver, wilder, more adult person. I was barreling through an "elite" prep school, where phrases like *Ivy League* and *permanent record* felt like they hung on the walls, and up to this point, I had been made to believe that anything bad I did would resurface to damage my future. No college wants a student who isn't perfect. No job wants a graduate from a shitty school. No man wants a woman with a worthless job. No woman wants to go through life without a man. More than math and science, I was learning these lessons in school.

But when I started to fail, those things began to lose their weight. I wasn't sure I wanted any of that or needed it to survive. I reveled in my new identity as someone who didn't care or try. After all, I was too wild for a real college and a real job and a good man to take care of me. I was never going to be as pretty or polished as the girls in my class were, with their duplex apartments in Jerry Seinfeld's building and highlights their mothers paid for. I was never going to be as smart as the kids whose brains could reason out matrices and polynomials. But maybe that was fine. I didn't need to be perfect if I was a rebel. Cool people lived by their own rules. I could live off acid and stolen fruits in Los Angeles, like my beloved Jim. Maybe the cycle of good schools and good jobs and good, dutiful offspring was something I was meant to break.

.

The thing about these fancy private schools is that they won't let you fail, no matter how hard you try. This, I suspect, has more to do with preserving their *U.S. News & World Report* rankings and steady stream of alumni donations than any real concern for their students, but it is what it is. Teachers at my school oversaw a small number of students in advisory groups, which meant there was someone paying attention to me when I went from a good student to a poor one.

My adviser, a former investment banker who now taught economics and history, wasn't actually all that attentive, and appeared to assume my silly girl brain had always been slow. But he did have a meeting with my parents to go over my report card, and since the two of them had believed for so long that their baby girl was a certified genius, they were quite surprised by the comments on my quarterly report suggesting I was not.

"What's going on with you?" my mother asked, after reading a note from my American history teacher suggesting I had not once opened the textbook. "Are you on drugs?"

"I'm not on drugs!" I insisted, though to my mother, smoking pot twice was the equivalent of running a cartel.

They did not understand what was wrong. But they knew something *was,* and their incredible disappointment radiated outward every time they looked at me. It turns out no matter how hard you try to be a new person, the old version of you refuses to go away, and the part of me that wanted my parents to love me for being good sent out panic signals. By attending this school, by letting other people shovel money into an education that was supposed to push me forward, I had been handed an opportunity. I was wasting it. I was ungrateful. I had strayed from the path, and now it was time to come back.

Several months of fucking around had rendered me academically rusty, and it appeared that if I wanted to pass tenth grade, I would have to give up the Jim Morrison videos and clove-smoking sessions and maybe read a book. When I started studying again, I got As in my good subjects. And with some diligence, I managed to get my math grade all the way up to a C+, a mark my college guidance counselor would later circle at each of our meetings when it came time to apply to my beloved Brown.

Tragically, I am not a genius. I did not get into Brown or any Ivy League institution, but I did just fine, even with my small dip in grades. In the world of the Manhattan rich, there is no such thing as failing, no matter how hard you try. Last I heard, Jake's parents bought him an apartment.

•

This was not the only time I let myself sink. In college, there were semesters in which I gave up, because life was more rewarding when I was out making a mess of it than when I was impressing TAs by memorizing *The Winter's Tale* (which I also did). There've been periods in adulthood—short periods, but they've existed—in which I've swapped out hard work and diligence for binge-drinking and reckless sexual encounters. I have spent money on cigarettes that I needed for my gas bill. I have done shots at eleven P.M. and called out sick at nine A.M. There have been mornings in which I look in the mirror, see my sunken eyes and yellowing skin, and know I am pickling myself from the inside.

But the rebellion never sticks. No matter how much

I flirt with the idea of letting things turn to shit, of breaking with who I am supposed to be, I always seem to pull myself out of free fall before I'm rendered bloodied and splayed out on the sidewalk.

Sometimes I am tired of being me. I am tired of the cycle. Even if I live my life on a parallel track—even if I technically didn't get a good moneymaking job or make good babies who will go to good schools to later make their own good money and babies—I am still on *a* track, and I am going to stay on it. Sometimes I want to know what it would be like if I weren't, if I didn't live up to expectations, if there were none to live up to at all. I wonder if I'd have any drive, or, as I suspect in dark moments, if left to my own devices, I would fail for real.

In these moments, I revisit my teen urge to toss the person I am most of the time—one who makes deadlines and gets sleep and doesn't fuck other people's boyfriends—in favor of a person who cares less. Sometimes I want to stop trying. Sometimes I want to see who I am when I am untethered. Who would I be if I didn't owe anything to anyone, if I had no one to impress and no one to disappoint? Who would I have been?

It's impossible to know. In the end, I always remember those I'm letting down, what I'm wasting, how hard everyone else worked to put me here and how little I deserve it. I am easily bored. I am spoiled as shit. I have been loved. People catch me when I fall.

Good Things Happen
to People You Hate

When I graduated from college, I got a job as a cashier at a popular clothing chain. We were paid almost nothing, and since landlords don't accept spandex dresses and chiffon blouses as rent, I ate stewed tomatoes straight out of the can for quite a few meals. But for a short period of time, it was the best job I ever had. I spent my shifts flirting with my hot hip musician coworkers and doing little else. At night, after we closed the store, we'd all do drugs and go to shows together at various now-shuttered Williamsburg DIY venues, whose other attendees were also employees at the clothing chain's other outposts. On my days off, I worked as an unpaid intern at a local magazine, where I fact-checked restaurant listings and complained about how I was too cool to be there. I got a lot of cute free clothes. Indeed, I was living the 2011 Brooklyn Dream, canned tomato dinners notwithstanding.

Still, there were some downsides to this laissez-faire life of music and fashion, besides poor nutrition. The store I worked at was on a wealthy stretch of the Upper East Side, which made for an eclectic customer base and a strong contrast with my current lifestyle. We got a lot of rich teen girls, many of whom liked to swarm the store in hordes and steal all the leggings. And we got a lot of the teen girls' rich mothers, who liked to buy the leggings and then yell at us about the return policy.

In the angry moms' defense, the policy was horrendous—the store permitted only exchanges or store credit, so once you handed them your money, they held it hostage forever. As cashiers, we tried to make this fact as clear as possible. "There are NO refunds," we'd say before swiping credit cards. "You will NEVER see this money again," we'd say after, while circling the small print at the bottom of the receipt. "Please note that your money is now DEAD, and this is its DEATH CERTIFICATE," we'd conclude, handing the customer a bag containing their new outfit. But inevitably, each day five or six people would try to get $20 back for a T-shirt, and we, the hapless employees earning $9 to $13 an hour, were responsible for absorbing their subsequent rage.

There was a stark difference between what we earned and what our customers were able to buy. People brought $400 worth of sweaters to the cash register for me to ring up (i.e., five or six sweaters). On Halloween, we were swarmed with people dropping major cash on shiny leotards and ballerina skirts they'd probably wear one time and toss. Later, at a Halloween party hosted by a college friend, I'd see other attendees wearing the clothes we sold. Each of their outfits cost more than I made in a day.

Once I went to a fancy bar in Brooklyn for a story I was doing for a magazine, on the magazine's dime. I noticed I was wearing the same pair of shiny "Olivia Newton-John in *Grease*" pants as another patron. The pants were ridiculous. I got them for free. She had bought them for $150.

I was very good at this job, in part because I never let anyone buy anything I knew they would hate and ultimately attempt to return. Salespeople, generally, are not to be trusted. A salesperson's job is to sell you stuff so they can pay their rent; your job as a customer is not to be an idiot and buy something you don't like just because a stranger said it looked nice on you.

But I never told anyone something looked good on them when it didn't, and usually offered (gentle) suggestions for items that might look better instead. If you think I did this out of some deep, impenetrable love for my clientele, you are quite wrong—mostly, I didn't want any rich middle-aged ladies coming back and screaming at me for letting them purchase a nonrefundable neon leotard. Life is too short to spend it listening to people threaten you over clothing regret.

Sometimes these efforts would fail, and customers still bought the items I tried to talk them out of, eventually returning to bellow at someone (hopefully not me!) about getting their money back. But for the most part, my commitment to honesty cultivated a sense of trust between my customers and me. They started coming back to the store specifically to buy stuff from me, which did wonders for my sales numbers and self-esteem, if not my actual bank account.

By spring, I'd been promoted to floor manager, which meant I was earning just enough money to add pasta to my stewed tomatoes. (It was also my first ever promotion, and I was very proud.) One day I was working behind the cash register shortly before closing time when a cool-looking woman in cool-looking glasses who appeared to be in her late twenties or early thirties came up to purchase a sweater dress.

"I'm a little worried about it," she confessed as she placed the sweater on the counter. "It looks like it's pilling already. Do you think it'll hold up?" The sweater dress in question was a new item, and though for the most part my store made clothes to last, I couldn't say for certain that this would follow suit. Since she'd asked, I told her as much. "I think it's a great sweater," I added.

"But we don't do refunds, which is something to keep in mind if it's something you're really not sure about."

"Are you trying to talk me out of a sale?" she said, her voice sharp. It was not the response I expected. I explained I was trying to make sure she didn't leave with something for which she couldn't get her money back. "I just want to know if you think it's going to hold up," she said. "It's not that hard a question."

"I'm sure it'll last the season," I offered, which at that point was the best my end-of-shift brain could do. It seemed to suffice, as she handed me her card to swipe. "Are you sure?" I asked, card poised over the reader. "Remember, I can't refund it." She said she was sure. I swiped.

"Actually, I don't want it," she said, the instant her receipt started printing. "Please refund it."

"But we don't do refunds!" I sputtered. "I don't care," she said. "You said it was only going to last the season. I'm not spending thirty dollars on something that only lasts one season."

My assistant manager was working that shift, so I offered to call her. "Yeah, you better," the customer, whose face I was starting to contemplate slamming on the register, said. "I'm going to tell her you tried to talk me out of the sale," she added. FACE. SLAM.

My assistant manager was relatively new to our store, and I wasn't sure how she'd react to this particular customer service snafu. When she came up from the downstairs office to ask what happened, I explained that this dumb bitch wanted a refund on her stupid fucking sweater, but not quite in those words. The customer started harping at her about me, which I was certain would result in some punishment. "It's her fault. She tried to talk me out of it!" she said, pointing at me. Then "'I'm sure it'll last the season,'" the woman said, in a voice I can only assume was a mocking approximation of mine.

By now I wanted to purchase the sweater myself and use its pilling yarn to strangle her to death. Instead, my assistant manager offered her a special secret refund that the store reserved for customers who yelled a lot about the return policy, because a fun fact about the service industry is that if you're a customer you can usually get what you want if you're enough of a jerk about it. Satisfied, and a full thumping $30 richer, the woman walked out. I waited for my boss to berate me. "What a bitch," my manager said, then headed back down to the office.

•

Sweater Lady wasn't the worst customer I had at that store or at other gigs I've worked that required me to be nice to people, but something about that interaction stamped itself on my psyche. I knew her name from her credit card, so I looked her up. I found out where she went to college—somewhere not as good as my alma mater, *not that it matters*—and that she had a cushy position at a bank, one that probably gave her enough cash to purchase a dozen $30 sweaters and toss them each season if she wanted.

I dreamed of this woman's destruction. I fucking hated her. She'd tried to get me in trouble, for one thing, but for another, she had the gall to make fun of me. At night, I rehashed her mocking tone. *Who the fuck does she think she was talking to?* I'd think. *Doesn't she know who I am?* Not that I *was* anybody at the time, but I was a *person*, dammit! And my voice wasn't *nearly* as high as the one she used to mimic me! I am an *alto*.

To her, I was some idiot salesgirl unworthy of her respect, and her refusal to see beyond my service position enraged me. She deserved nothing short of eternal suffering. I wanted her to lose her job, get dumped, fall through a subway grate, have her identity stolen, battle a roach infestation, get evicted, and generally live a miserable life. I meanwhile would one day grow up to be rich and famous, and one day we'd run into each other, and I'd rub in how magnificent I had become while she'd devolved into a pathetic trash human. I vowed to never forget her. I vowed to hurt her.

•

Sweater Lady wasn't the first object of my thirst for ven-geance. One summer I went to a sleepaway camp where the girls were baffled by my frizzy hair, cheap jeans, and dog T-shirts. They were troubled when they discovered my family owned only two televisions and one computer. "Do your parents have money for your college educa-tion?" one girl asked me one night. "Can they afford to buy you a hairbrush?" When I got home, after forcing my mother to take me to Abercrombie & Fitch and pur-chase me a lifetime supply of LA Looks gel, I cursed my bunkmates, hoping the mean girls would grow up to be ugly and sad, with zero televisions to their name.

Indeed, I wanted everyone who wronged me to suf-fer karmic retribution. When a boy I loved in college dropped me the week before our freshman finals, I cursed him with future miserable relationships. When a man broke my heart years later, I hoped his hairline would recede. When a friend stabbed me in the back and stole a boy I liked out from under me, I prayed for her to be hit with adult onset acne. When I read, while waiting for the bus in the rain, that Lindsay Lohan said in an interview that her favorite body part was her nose, I begged for her to be struck with syphilis. My small miseries at their behest still burned, but I knew it was nothing next to the anguish the universe would bestow upon them in the end.

In a world where you have little control and everyone else's successes light up your social media feeds, revenge fantasies are a great source of empowerment. It's no coincidence that superhero comics started emerging at the end of the Great Depression and the start of World War II. It's even less of a coincidence that Marvel started pumping out *Avengers* films amid the twenty-first century's interminable economic and political turmoil. In times of uncertainty, people take comfort in watching the good guys vanquish their enemies.

On the night Donald Trump was elected, I was at Hillary Clinton's presumptive victory party at the Javits Center in New York. I'd been sent there for work—reluctantly, since all I really wanted was to be surrounded by my friends and wine bottles in case the night didn't go the way I hoped it would. At six P.M., my biggest complaint was that there was no bar and the few food vendors on hand were charging $13 for baked ziti; but when Florida started to flip, I hightailed it out of there like the Dedicated Journalist I am, choosing instead to watch the *New York Times* prediction widget have a meltdown from the safety of my best friend's living room.

For months afterward, I couldn't stop thinking about violence. In my daydreams, members of Congress were flipped inside out like the giant pig alien in *Galaxy Quest.* I chopped up their bodies and fed them to their children. I lit their feet on fire and watched their limbs turn to ash in the flames. House Speakers with disintegrating faces danced in my peripheral vision. CNN made me so angry that the receptors in my eyes went dark. My blood pressure spiked from a pretty chill 110/70 to 130/110, which was high enough for my doctor to suggest coming back regularly to get it checked. (I solved that problem by never going back to the doctor.) I typed up tweets I never sent, for fear the Secret Service would mistake my blind rage for a call to action and pay me a visit. My roommate and I watched *V for Vendetta* and plotted elaborate ways to take down our leaders if we did indeed descend into George Orwell–esque fascism.

To be clear, these were all just fantasies, but they kept me from sinking into despair. I know what it says about me that I didn't experience this kind of existential panic until Trump's election, but for the first time in my very silly charmed life, I had to come to terms with the fact that things weren't guaranteed to be okay. It was unfathomable to me at the time that the hot president who tried to give us health care had been swapped out for a racist orange blob with a Twitter addiction. I was angry, and I wanted to dream about violence, because violence was the only way to stop feeling scared.

Three years in, this societal thirst for revenge feels like it's everywhere. The internet is full of people screaming at one another into the void. Family members threaten excommunication. Television channels and newspapers and verified conspiracy theorists on Twitter run story after story hinting at treason, vast webs of deceit, manipulation by a foreign power, the promise of impeachment, of dragging the bad guys out of the White House by their heels. People lap these stories up. They want proof this isn't real. They want proof the so-called Good Guys will win. It doesn't come.

•

Revenge, in real life, has not been forthcoming. The camp girls that made me feel bad are all beautiful and married with babies whose photographs they splatter all over Instagram, while my feed consists primarily of my selfies, because I am my own baby. Most of my former paramours didn't lose their hair; even if they did, most of them have hot significant others and careers they appear to tolerate, while I fuse to my couch eating suspicious Hostess bodega snacks and avoiding emails with the words *CREDIT CARD STATEMENT* in the subject line.

When my journalist friends lost their jobs, the people who sold out their companies landed on their feet, with money in the bank, while everyone else scrounged for freelance gigs and sublet their apartments so they wouldn't have to pay New York rents on $300-per-story budgets. The billionaire who shut down my website has yet to be gored by bison, no matter how many times I screamed bloody murder about it in a bar. The congressmen I wish pain upon appear to be doing just fine. I have not yet heard of one ingesting his child. At least Lindsay Lohan doesn't seem to be doing so hot, though her nose still looks like it's holding up, despite her best efforts.

The cliché people spout about revenge is true—the best revenge *is*, in fact, living well, which is a difficult thing to do when you feel like your life is falling apart all the time. Revenge fantasies make your own personal hell feel a little less hellish, but like chocolate and orgasms, the thrill is fleeting. Ultimately, living well means ceding control. Not caring requires you to give yourself up to the universe, instead of flinging your enemies into the vortex.

This is a true fact in many different forms. Every time I've severed ties with a toxic friend or a toxic man (often one and the same), I've wanted them to miss me, but all I can really do is kick them out of my life long enough to stop missing *them*—everything else is out of my hands. The universe tends to unfold as it should, as they say, but not because it doles out punishments. It's because you forget.

There's also this. No one is bad, and we all are. I've hurt plenty of people along the way, but I don't think of them, and my enemies don't think of me.

•

The Sweater Lady incident happened nearly a decade ago, and in the intervening years, I've since forgotten her real name, even though I swore I'd remember it forever. I have no idea if my miserable customer ended up with the terrible life I tried to curse her with. I don't know if she lost her job or her boyfriend or her friends or her eye when someone finally punched her in the face and shattered her stupid glasses into her cornea. I will probably never know.

And I didn't turn into the super successful, super happy bombshell I hoped I'd taunt her with one day. On the other hand, I left the store and got some jobs and lost some jobs and bought my own pilling sweaters and generally had enough adventures and mishaps and wild nights in my intervening life to mostly forget about hers, which for the most part is the best you can do. Over time Sweater Lady will fade even further, and one day she'll be gone.

But if you happen to be Sweater Lady and you're reading this very essay, know this: I think you're a bitch. Have a nice life.

Summer of Death

A dead body doesn't look the way they tell you it will. I have never been to a wake or an open casket funeral—my people prefer to keep dead bodies sealed in boxes where they belong, thank you very much—but I have seen a dead body. From what I've heard, the IRL *Six Feet Under* crew cakes bodies with makeup and dresses them so they look like sleeping wax dolls. I assume this is not to disturb the breathing people who come to view the bodies, because real bodies that are no longer living don't look like dolls or sleeping people. They look dead. The look is unmistakable.

I grew up in a city where dead bodies were probably everywhere, but I never bothered to look at them. I remember seeing still, frozen bodies on the street in the winter. I saw a bloodied body get pulled out of a cab, and I once saw a body on a subway grate. These were strange bodies. They belonged to people who did not belong to me, so I did not think about them often, even when, on at least one occasion, I saw a canvas-covered body get rolled away on a gurney and knew for certain what that meant.

Last summer for the first time I saw a body that once belonged to a person I loved. The body was my grandmother's, and it sat still in her bed at her house in Cold Spring, New York, on the morning of July 3. At the time, I was alone at the house with my maternal grandparents. I had just finished brushing my teeth when my grandfather came into my room to get me. I opened my mouth to tell him he should have knocked. "There's something wrong with Bunny," he said. I closed my mouth, opened it again, and said, "Okay." I followed him into their bedroom, and there was her shed skin, a silent yellow-gray molt sitting stiff and supine in the spot where just hours earlier there had been a pink and breathing person.

•

A month before I saw my grandmother's body, Anthony Bourdain died and I entered an inexplicable period of mourning. It was a strange reaction for me to have, since though I'd always liked Bourdain's interviews and

Twitter account (which gifted us with gems like "I'm doing a Kickstarter to buy Ted Cruz a Fleshlight"), I was not a fangirl. I'd never read *Kitchen Confidential* and I'd seen only a handful of episodes of his two big shows. Bourdain had a name and a face that I recognized, but I didn't really know him at all.

And yet his death struck through me like a fever. I became a woman obsessed. I watched every episode of *Parts Unknown* and *No Reservations,* and every clip from every late-night interview. I scrolled through his tweets as far back as the archives permitted. I read article after article after article, pre- and postmortem, so I could sit inside his life for a minute. I lay awake at night and cried, and in the morning, I woke up drenched in sweat and the sense that something in the universe as I knew it was amiss.

I am always upset when celebrities die because in my sad made-up world, I know them as intimately as I know my own friends. When Heath Ledger died, I was so startled I spent $200 on empire waist dresses at Urban Outfitters. I cried over Philip Seymour Hoffman. You will need to come collect me when Harrison Ford kicks it.

But this inexplicable obsession was intense in a different way, maybe because of this: Bourdain looks exactly like my father. Perhaps *exactly* is a strong word, since Bourdain was six-four and my father is decidedly not.

But they are both half Jewish and half Mediterranean (Bourdain's father is from the South of France, while my paternal grandmother's family is from Southern Italy) with curly salt-and-pepper hair. They have similar bone structures, and the skin on their faces creases in the same spots. In certain photos, the resemblance is uncanny. They are alike in other ways, too—they both had wild pasts, are older fathers, and boast a gruffness burying a secret sweetness you have to earn.

When I watched Bourdain navigate new cities on *Parts Unknown,* I searched for familiar side angles and glimpses of my father's face in his. When he died, it struck a chord, a reminder of an inevitability that I largely keep out of view.

•

The day after the Bourdain news broke, some friends and I went to see a horror movie called *Hereditary.* I love horror movies because I hate them. After I saw *The Ring,* I wouldn't sleep in a room with a television in it for months. But I am a masochist and I love to torture my brain, so I bought tickets in advance for this film, which critics were calling "uncommonly unsettling" and "the scariest movie in years." I was ready for terror.

Unfortunately, though *Hereditary* was marketed as a spooky ghost flick, the real horror is rooted too much in reality to make it fun. For the sake of no spoilers, I won't disclose exactly what happens, but know that about half an hour into the film, there is a significant death. The death scene is shot in such a way that you, an audience member who bought a ticket to this aya-huasca trip because you thought you'd just be dealing with jump scares and Casper, are forced to sit with and process this death along with the bereaved. You are forced to think—for several minutes, in brutal silence—about how you would feel if you saw some-one you loved die violently, what it would be like to know you and your life were changed forever, and that nothing was ever again going to be or feel okay.

I tend to leave horror films haunted by shadows in my room and breezes in the shower, but I left this one haunted by death. I was already grieving Bourdain and my not-dead father and now I grieved everyone. What would I do if my sister died in an accident? How would I process the loss of my best friend? What was I going to remember about my mother? If the men I'd once loved succumbed all of a sudden, was I allowed to cry?

Death was everywhere, and now it was in my brain. I could not stop thinking about it, I could not stop fearing it, and I could not stop seeing the people I loved lying lifeless on a slab. And then, a few weeks later, there was my grandmother, dead in her bed.

•

I decided early on in the summer that I would spend the first week of July at my grandparents' house with them. I had just started writing this very book, and though New York City is a good muse for writers, in part because of the crush of people and also because of the subway horror tales, all the great stories the city feeds you while you're living here tend to distract you from actually writing them down. My grandparents split their time between Cold Spring and their rent-stabilized apartment on the Upper West Side (OH, TO HAVE LIVED AND LOVED IN THE 1960s), and though they offered me their house when they were in the city, I decided to pick a week when we'd all be together. The Good Granddaughter version of me said this was because the two of them were having trouble navigating steps, and I wanted to help them out. The Selfish Granddaughter chose that week because I had never in my entire life spent a night alone in a house, and I was scared. I'm not sure which version had the final say.

I am not a great driver and my grandmother was not great at stocking a fridge with unexpired food, so my parents offered to ferry me up to Cold Spring, buy us some groceries (I am very spoiled), and spend the night before heading back into Manhattan. When I showed up at their apartment for my free ride, though, they informed me they'd be driving back to the city after dropping me off. My sister was sick, and she was crashing at their place until she felt better. We are both very spoiled.

"We don't want to leave her," my mother said, so instead they were going to leave me. We made it to Cold Spring, but when we got to town, my father discovered a bubble in his tire, so they left right away, dropping me at the house before heading to an auto shop in hopes of staving off a fatal blowout on the West Side Highway. As I watched them pull out of the parking lot, I felt a sudden stab of longing, a sense that I was being left alone. I wanted to run after their car and ask them to stay. This was strange. I am an adult. It is easier for me to spend less time with my parents, not more, because I can drink as much soda as I want and no one tells me when to go to bed. And yet I did not want them to go.

This was not the first time my mother's parents and I were spending time alone together. We grew up as much with them as we did with my real parents. When my sister and I were little, my grandparents babysat us often, feeding us ice cream and letting us stay up late to watch old movies (much, I presume, to my parents' delight, when two very cranky children were dropped at their doorstep in the morning).

My grandmother and I had monthly lunch dates. She loved art, theater, and fashion, so we went to museums and Broadway shows and fought endlessly in clothing stores because she refused to believe I didn't look good in gauchos. We went to the movies and sat in her living room and drank tea, and she told me she was glad I talked to her about real things, not just the weather and school, as grandchildren who treated their grandparents like obligations did. We were so close we could argue, but not so close our fights were as vicious as the ones I have with my mother. My grandmother was much more concerned about the coat I wouldn't zip up than about whether I'd grow up to reflect all the things in her she didn't like.

But on this particular hot day in July, the instant my parents pulled out of the parking lot, my nerves started shredding. It was very hot. It was at least 90 degrees, with a delightful mid-Atlantic 1000 percent humidity, and the old house had air conditioning in only two rooms. My grandmother kept complaining about the heat, but she refused to wear a short-sleeved shirt. I told her to sit in a room with AC, but she kept wandering around the subtropical kitchen instead. "It's so hot," she said. "Why are you wearing a sweater?" I asked. "It's not a sweater," she said. It was, but she wasn't going to change.

All this sounds like a warning shot, and considering what happened next, it should have been. But my grandmother loved to complain almost as much as she loved the Metropolitan Museum of Art and telling me to put on lipstick. She was upright and elegant and doctors said she was in mostly perfect health, though she spent a decade claiming she was nearly dead. My sister likes to tell a story about going to the theater with my grandmother a few years ago. They were in line for headphones, right behind a woman with a walker who was wrinkled, bent over, and essentially crumbling, and she apologized to my grandmother after bumping into her. "We're in the same boat, you and I," my straight-backed grandmother told her, pointing to the cane she carried with her but somehow never let touch the ground. The woman looked at her in disbelief.

(She complained about more than just aging. One time I was walking with her on Columbus Avenue on the tony Upper West Side when she jabbed at a single small crack in the sidewalk. "You see that?" she hissed. "*De Blasio*," referencing the much-maligned mayor of New York. My grandmother was very political.)

So my grandmother's complaints didn't seem out of the ordinary, and I didn't have the energy to fight her. I was starting to think staying in Cold Spring was a mistake. The heat was so intense I couldn't bend my fingers. It was the kind of hot that makes you feel like you're trapped in a box, like you're suffocating, like you're having a panic attack and there is no respite. I wanted to go home. My landlord had not gotten back to us about our lease renewal, and I was worried the new rent would be too high. My friends had July Fourth drinking plans, pre–July Fourth drinking plans, and post–July Fourth drinking plans, and I was going to miss all of them. I had struck up a flirtation with a man in the city, and now I was far away from him. I wanted the week to end. It was only Saturday.

·

On Sunday night, my grandmother started screaming that she thought there was something wrong with her. My grandfather called her doctor, and on Monday morning, they drove back to the city. She's fine, the doctor assured them. It's just the heat. My mother urged them to stay in the city, where air conditioning was plentiful. I wanted them to stay in the city, too. The house was peaceful without them. I got a lot of work done. I liked having all the rooms to myself. But they insisted on coming back. That night I drove them to dinner, worrying the whole time that I'd crash the car into a pole or a deer or twelve deer and kill us all. But we made it and drove back, and I said good night to them. In the morning, my grandmother was dead.

·

Like turning off a light in a familiar room, it takes a minute for your eyes to adjust to a dead body that once belonged to someone you loved. The outline is there, yes, but the details are all wrong. The body is still and silent, like an object, like a table, like nothing. The skin doesn't twitch or heave or even minutely pulse. This sounds obvious—of course someone who is dead cannot move—but it is startling to see it for yourself in inaction. And you know death when you see it. You know immediately that the person who was once in that body has gotten out of it, even if you yell their name and shake them and ask them very desperately to wake up.

I have never believed in the afterlife. The idea of spending an eternity in heaven seems just as unpleasant as spending an eternity on earth. Nothing is ever good forever. I always liked the idea of reincarnation, if just because it fed my desire to experience life as a different person or a bird, because I would love to peck out all my enemies' eyes.

But when I saw the Nana-skin, I started to suspect whatever was once inside had to go somewhere. Sure, science says life is just blood circulating and some brain activity, but if that's the case, why did the Nana-skin look so empty? How is it just organs that make a person smile and laugh and breathe and go "camping" with you under the dining room table? Was it just mitral and tricuspid valves that sewed your rag doll a new face after you destroyed the old one with too much love and toddler snot? Are oxygenated blood cells responsible for bandaging your bruises and hugging you when you cried and telling you they loved you even though you simply *refused* to try on those gauchos?

The thing in the bed was not my grandmother. It was a pile of bones and flesh, but there was nothing inside. The paramedics came and confirmed it was a body and not a person. The body got picked up by the funeral home and driven back to the city. It got put in a cold drawer in the funeral home, where my mother and aunt looked at it and confirmed what it once had been. It got put in a box that we rolled down the aisle at a standing-room-only funeral in a 300-capacity hall. It got driven to a cemetery in Westchester, and then it got put in the ground. And the rest of us, the living, drove back to Manhattan without it.

•

When an elderly person dies, grieving feels like an unnecessary indulgence. People are supposed to die when they are old. My father's mother was much older than my mother's parents, and when we visited her in her musty apartment in Brooklyn, she cried when we tried to leave. In her nineties, she lived for Rice Krispies cereal, *Wheel of Fortune*, and intermittent visits from family members who didn't really want to be there. When she died at age ninety-three, I was almost happy for her.

And so I have felt strange, grieving for my

grandmother—perhaps even stranger than I did in grieving for Bourdain, a person I did not know but who was not supposed to die. I don't think I deserve to be as sad as I am. I don't think I'm allowed to listen to a voice mail she left me in April and sit down on the street. I'm not even sure that when she left it, I remembered to call her back. But this is not a story about mourning. It is a story about death.

It sounds like this was my first experience with death, but it was not. Death has always been around me, because it is always around everyone. My father's best friend died of a heart attack when I was nine. I remember going to shiva at their apartment and eating cake and sitting in his eighteen-year-old daughter's room, giggling when someone asked me if I wanted a cigarette. The father of two children I babysat for in high school dropped dead one day at work. The mother of a little girl I tutored died by suicide. A twenty-year-old girl in my roommates' sorority was killed by a driver while walking to the campus one morning. Family friends and family members and friends I had but lost touch with have died. Often these were people who were young and strong and who were not supposed to die.

But I did not see their bodies. I know what I'm looking for now. My parents will die. My sister will die. My friends will die. You and I and everyone we love and hate and meet and walk by on the street and sit next to on the train will die. If I feared looking at their lifeless bodies before, I fear it even more now. I can see them stepping out of their bodies, leaving the rest of us with empty gray piles of aged tendon and skin. This will happen again and again and again and again and again. If we're lucky. Maybe we won't be. Maybe the Arctic will melt, the sea levels will rise, the Earth will run out of food, oxygen, water, sun. Maybe it won't, but we'll all die anyway.

I Went to South America
to Find Myself and All I Found
Was a Forty-Foot Jesus

Handel's *Messiah* boomed from speakers hidden in the plastic mountain, while we, the onlookers, huddled atop bleachers about twenty feet away. It was a perfect early March day in Argentina, with a soft breeze and sunshine so abundant my friend Lauren and I had to shade our eyes, even though it was already late afternoon. As we strained to see the mountain from our perch, we could hear children squeal in Spanish as they climbed a pack of plastic camels to our right. I was tired. We'd been at the park for hours and I was ready to go back to the hostel. It was my second-to-last full day in Buenos Aires, and I wanted a nap and a steak before I had to pack. I was not looking forward to going home, not that my new post-fire apartment, which I'd moved into just a couple months prior, felt much like one. I did not want to go back to work, which now seemed exclusively populated by men who had seen me naked. But my trip was almost over, and thus loomed the inevitable.

It was Handel that pulled me out of my fatigued reverie. The music drew my attention to the brown plastic mass that had started creeping out of the rock. First, there was a plastic forehead; then plastic eyebrows, plastic eyes, a hint of plastic ear.

•

The site of this baffling plastic resurrection was Tierra Santa, a Bible-themed amusement park for children located right by Buenos Aires's domestic airport. Tierra Santa means Holy Land, and certainly it is thus—in fact, it is set up to evoke biblical Jerusalem, permitting visitors to walk where Jesus walked and experience his life through his eyes, provided he lived his life in tiny plastic dioramas populated by his clones. You can climb Golgotha, the hill where Jesus hung on the cross, and indeed, there are the three life-size bloodless plastic dead bodies hanging atop the plastic rock.

You can see Roman soldiers flogging Jesus outside the plastic Temple in Jerusalem, which, yes, has also been re-created for your personal enjoyment. You can see plastic Jesus carrying the plastic cross through town, plastic blood on his chest and dripping on the ground in his wake. You can also visit other people and places in biblical history. There's a plastic Lazarus, freshly risen from the dead and looking like it. There's plastic Pontius Pilate, happy to greet you in his fancy plastic Roman temple. There are plastic examples of other houses of worship, including a plastic Muslim mosque that is at least vaguely if not openly racist. And all of this is for children! It is magnificent.

What started out as an impulsive trip below the border was fast transforming into a pilgrimage, and I didn't hate it.

•

I decided to go to Argentina on a whim. When my apartment building caught fire—forcing me and my few remaining possessions to briefly move in with my parents—shit got unsettled. I was now a new person, with new clothes and a newfound appreciation for renters insurance and the FDNY. I found a new apartment, but it meant I would move to a strange neighborhood with two strange people, living in a strange room with a strange empty bookshelf and a strange empty set of drawers. And other things were new. There was a boy I knew well, had liked, and thought liked me. But after I slept with him a few times, he dropped me, and now he was strange to me, too.

I never much liked change. For me, it always

seemed like a threat, like a sign that when things were good they would assuredly turn bad. But after the fire, change seemed like something to embrace. It was nice to no longer feel tied down to old shit. Things change all the time, and if they could change for the worse, that also meant there was room for them to change for the better. Perhaps the new me, with new clothes and a new home and no too-tight Urban Outfitters dresses around to weigh me down would be braver, smarter, hotter, cooler, wiser, happier. But several months into the newness, everything still felt miserable.

I did not know the new me very well yet when I made the call to take her on a test drive to a new hemisphere. My friend Lauren is much braver than me, and in January 2016, she quit her job at our website and booked a one-way ticket to Peru, whereupon she planned to spend three months traveling solo through South America. I could not fathom doing anything as courageous as this, considering how often I get turned around when I exit my very own subway station.

But in January 2016, I needed a journey, a way to test my new sea legs and the sneakers I bought to replace the old ones doused in toxic smoke. And I needed a brief escape—from New York, from subway blogs, from my tiny new room, from a job that now seemed composed of men who'd rejected me. Lauren told me to come visit her, and though pre-fire me couldn't make the effort to get to Philadelphia, let alone South America, the new me used the money I'd saved on rent from living at home to book a flight to Buenos Aires.

A thing about traveling in South America is that North Americans tend to do it in big chunks. It is far away and there is a lot to see, so people quit jobs, take sabbaticals, buy big backpacks, and hostel-hop their way through Peru, Ecuador, Bolivia, Argentina, and Chile for months at a time. They all do ayahuasca. They all take photos of themselves jumping for joy in the salt flats, a dried-out prehistoric lake in southwest Bolivia. They all return and claim they are now "fluent" in Spanish and have a newfound "appreciation" for Earth. I know several people who have done this exact trip. Not one has brought me back an alpaca. I am bitter.

The point is, it was not especially intrepid for me to meet a friend for a week of mayhem in a major metropolis. But I am not the sort of person who buys an $1,100 plane ticket only one month in advance, and I do not tend to fly halfway across the world to spend a week with someone I had worked with and often drank with but otherwise did not know very well. For me, this was as good as an adventure got. I hoped it would teach me something. I had, after all, once seen *Eat Pray Love* (coincidentally, on a plane).

•

Adventures never quite go the way you think they will, especially when they are backdropped by a lot of Fernet, which we drank like water. Here are some things I did in Buenos Aires:

- I spent two hours in the airport after my flight landed because I did not listen to my mother and therefore did not get Argentinian pesos before I left. Only one ATM at the airport worked and it took me several lifetimes to find it. (My mother will hold this over me forever.)
- On our first night in Buenos Aires, someone swiped Lauren's iPhone at a concert venue. Good thing she had only *one full month* of solo travel left.
- On our second night, a sailor from New Zealand tried to flirt with me by accusing the United States of doing military war crimes. He was technically correct, but it turns out in the Obama era I became very patriotic when drunk (on Fernet), and I argued with him until he slunk away. I would come to regret this later.
- On our third day, Lauren and I went to Tigre, a town just north of Buenos Aires that sits near the famous Paraná Delta. The big thing to do there is to take a boat ride to the delta, but the only available boat was in the late afternoon, several hours away. To kill

time, we walked around and went to a casino, where we won eight Argentinian pesos. Then we finally got on the boat and instantly fell asleep.

- On our fourth day, Lauren and I decided to take a vacation from our vacation, so we took the ferry to Colonia del Sacramento, a city in southwestern Uruguay with a bunch of old buildings and not much else. Our hostel had bedbugs. We got lost on a bike ride.
- On our fifth day, we returned to Buenos Aires to find ourselves booked into a hostel room with three sets of triple bunk beds, each of which threatened to sway and crumble every time one of its inhabitants moved or rustled or breathed.
- On our sixth day, we decided to have a "wild" night out, so we got in a cab and told the driver to take us to a club. He did. The club was called Brooklyn. There were subway signs and pictures of the Brooklyn Bridge on all the walls. Everyone was fifteen.

To sum up, things were not going according to plan. I hadn't learned very much about myself, other than that I liked Fernet a lot and had a habit of scaring off would-be suitors. I had not found true love or self-acceptance or a showstopping leather jacket. I was still going home to an alien apartment, to owning only two books, to a boy who had hurt me, to a job that was starting to strip me of my energy and, according to at least one optometrist, my eyesight. It did not seem like things were going to be okay.

But we had one more journey to take, one that would prove far more life-changing than anything that happened on the rest of the trip—we were going to Tierra Santa.

I had been begging Lauren to go to Tierra Santa since I got off the plane. I came across it during the thirteen seconds I spent preparing for this trip (i.e., googling "things to do in Buenos Aires." See also la República de los Niños, an amusement park about "democracy" where children can learn how to apply for bank loans. Also real! I did not get to go there.). I love theme parks, I love historical villages, I love kitsch, and I love things that are wildly inappropriate for kids and yet are somehow geared toward them. It was clear this was going to be my shit.

So finally, on my second-to-last day in town, we breached Tierra Santa's beautiful plastic gate.

•

Tierra Santa was, indeed, my Shangri-la. We went to an "interactive show" about the Genesis, in which decades-old animatronic animals and what looked like sex dolls repurposed as Adam and Eve appeared onstage in flashes of strobe light, the many schoolchildren in the audience cheering when they saw Eve's boobs. We went to another "interactive show" about the Last Supper, where animatronic Jesus and Judas each moved their head and one arm exactly one time, and nothing else happened.

We walked through at least three plastic nativity scenes, visited Noah's plastic ark, and snapped photos by the plastic Western Wall. We saw plastic donkeys and plastic Romans and plastic odes to Pope John Paul II, Gandhi, and Mother Teresa, whom I do not recall existing in the Bible, but perhaps I missed them. We saw many bloody plastic Jesuses. We considered purchasing some of the (allegedly nonplastic) Middle Eastern food that costumed employees hawked in the food court, but passed when we saw the prices. You could also buy burgers and pizza, just like the Apostles did in high school.

We spent several hours wandering the plastic grounds, shading ourselves under the plastic palm trees dotting the plastic biblical kingdom. But by late afternoon the crowd thinned and we were ready to go home. There's only so much shirtless, bleeding, plastic Jesus a person can take in one day, after all. As we made our way toward the exit, we saw a group of people huddled together, pointing to the plastic Golgotha just across the road. Then we heard it: Handel's *Messiah.*

As the music swelled, a figure started creeping out

of the mountain, and when his nose crested its apex, we knew what we were looking at: it was Jesus.

A forty-foot Jesus, in fact, who rose from the rock with such lethargy I thought the two-hour concerto might end before he made it out. At last the bottom of Jesus's plastic white robes peeked out above the plastic mountaintop, and there he was, in all his glory. "*Hallelujah!*" Handel's chorus crowed as Jesus closed his eyes and opened them, approximating what I can only assume was a very slow animatronic blink. "*Hallelujah!*" Jesus's arms lifted with the speed of a geriatric sloth. He turned his hands out and opened his palms. You could hear the motor parts creak from our perch, despite the many-yard distance. "*Hallelujah!*" He closed his palms again. *Messiah* continued to blast. I pulled out my phone camera. The nuns near me appeared to be crying. "This is *so fucking funny,*" someone next to me screamed.

It is hard to describe quite what it's like to watch a giant plastic Jesus—clad in giant plastic robes, with a giant plastic halo attached to his giant plastic head—mushroom out of a giant plastic mountain like an oversize whack-a-mole while nuns cry and children cheer. Truly, there is nothing like it. I laughed so hard the video I took looks like it belongs in *The Blair Witch Project.* I think the face wrinkles I made that day still live somewhere near my eyes.

But as quickly as Jesus appeared—that is to say, not quickly at all—he drew down his arms and sank back into the rock, where he would rest until the show began in another hour.

We left Tierra Santa, and a day and a half later I left Buenos Aires, buoyed by the memory of my visit to plastic biblical Jerusalem. I did not find adventure, bliss, or a boyfriend, or even a replacement for my smoke-damaged belongings or a job that didn't make me want to die sometimes. The new me was much like the old me—drunk and dumb and bedbug-prone and terrifying to men from all corners of the earth. Perhaps it would always be like this. Perhaps I would always be the same. Perhaps I would have to learn to seek bliss elsewhere, or accept it was something I'd never attain for long but experience in moments as fleeting as a forty-foot animatronic Jesus rising from a plastic rock in a children's amusement park. But at least I found that. And for those fleeting animatronic moments, everything felt okay.

Acknowledgments

I cannot heap enough thanks and praise upon Sarah Smith, my agent, and Emma Brodie, my editor at William Morrow, without whom this book would still be a collection of unhinged journal entries. Their patience and guidance (and Emma's staggeringly good edits) made this whole process infinitely better. It was a pleasure to work with both of them.

To the rest of the team at William Morrow—Liate Stehlik, Cassie Jones, Ben Steinberg, Rachel Weinick, Owen Corrigan, Eliza Rosenberry, Jes Lyons, and Lauren Lauzon—thank you so much for helping me put the inside of my brain on paper, and for trying to sell it. I don't know why you would agree to do this, but I'm glad you did.

Thank you to Lauren Evans, who accompanied me on far too many of these misadventures, and without whom I would be a much less interesting person. Thank you to Dave Colon, who has let me cry in his apartment at least twice. Thank you to John Del Signore, who made me a better writer, and to Emma Whitford, Nell Casey, and Fraylie Nord.

To Molly Dillon, Christina Padilla, Emma Alterman, Ariella Cohain, Dan Hochman, Alex Finkel, and Remy Nelson—I'm sorry for all the late-night panic texts and phone calls, but I love you all very much.

Thank you to my grandmother, Bunny Hoffinger, whom I miss every single day.

And endless and eternal thanks to Fran, Harvey, and Alice, who have put up with a lot and yet still seem to love me.

About the Author

REBECCA FISHBEIN is a former senior editor at Gothamist and a current writer/television addict. She was born and raised in Manhattan, where at the tender age of two she ate her first H&H bagel. It's all been downhill from there. She graduated from the Johns Hopkins University Writing Seminars program, and has been published in *Baltimore City Paper*, *Time Out New York*, Jezebel, Vice, Splinter, *Adweek*, The Cut, Lifehacker, and Curbed NY, among other outlets. She lives in Brooklyn, New York.